ROLE BALDOCK is the proud
dren, all in good working order, a
light attention), a computer and
in 1993, she has worked a
and is a regular contributor to a variet
including American journals and the ̶ ̶ ̶ ̶ ̶ Britann-
ica. Editor of *Writing Competitions Monthly* and associate
editor of *Orbis*, she has written several schools information packs as well as being author of *Writing Reviews* and
Making Money from Writing.

Overcoming Common Problems Series

For a full list of titles please contact
Sheldon Press, Marylebone Road, London NW1 4DU

The Assertiveness Workbook
A plan for busy women
JOANNA GUTMANN

Beating the Comfort Trap
DR WINDY DRYDEN AND JACK
GORDON

Birth Over Thirty Five
SHEILA KITZINGER

Body Language
How to read others' thoughts by their
gestures
ALLAN PEASE

Body Language in Relationships
DAVID COHEN

Calm Down
How to cope with frustration and anger
DR PAUL HAUCK

Cancer – A Family Affair
NEVILLE SHONE

The Candida Diet Book
KAREN BRODY

Caring for Your Elderly Parent
JULIA BURTON-JONES

Cider Vinegar
MARGARET HILLS

Comfort for Depression
JANET HORWOOD

Coping Successfully with Hayfever
DR ROBERT YOUNGSON

**Coping Successfully with Joint
Replacement**
DR TOM SMITH

Coping Successfully with Migraine
SUE DYSON

Coping Successfully with Pain
NEVILLE SHONE

Coping Successfully with Panic Attacks
SHIRLEY TRICKETT

Coping Successfully with PMS
KAREN EVENNETT

**Coping Successfully with Prostate
Problems**
ROSY REYNOLDS

**Coping Successfully with Your Hiatus
Hernia**
DR TOM SMITH

**Coping Successfully with Your Irritable
Bowel**
ROSEMARY NICOL

**Coping Successfully with Your Irritable
Bladder**
JENNIFER HUNT

Coping with Anxiety and Depression
SHIRLEY TRICKETT

Coping with Blushing
DR ROBERT EDELMANN

Coping with Breast Cancer
DR EADIE HEYDERMAN

Coping with Bronchitis and Emphysema
DR TOM SMITH

Coping with Candida
SHIRLEY TRICKETT

Coping with Chronic Fatigue
TRUDIE CHALDER

Coping with Coeliac Disease
KAREN BRODY

Coping with Cystitis
CAROLINE CLAYTON

Coping with Depression and Elation
DR PATRICK McKEON

Coping with Eczema
DR ROBERT YOUNGSON

Coping with Endometriosis
JO MEARS

Coping with Fibroids
MARY-CLAIRE MASON

Coping with a Hernia
DR DAVID DELVIN

Coping with Psoriasis
PROFESSOR RONALD MARKS

Coping with Rheumatism and Arthritis
DR ROBERT YOUNGSON

Coping with Stammering
DR TRUDY STEWART AND JACKIE
TURNBULL

Coping with Stomach Ulcers
DR TOM SMITH

Overcoming Common Problems Series

Coping with Thrush
CAROLINE CLAYTON

Coping with Thyroid Problems
DR JOAN GOMEZ

Coping with Your Cervical Smear
KAREN EVENNETT

Crunch Points for Couples
JULIA COLE

Curing Arthritis
More ways to a drug-free life
MARGARET HILLS

Curing Arthritis Diet Book
MARGARET HILLS

Curing Arthritis – The Drug-Free Way
MARGARET HILLS

Curing Arthritis Exercise Book
MARGARET HILLS AND JANET
HORWOOD

Depression
DR PAUL HAUCK

Divorce and Separation
Every woman's guide to a new life
ANGELA WILLANS

**Everything Parents Should Know About
Drugs**
SARAH LAWSON

Feverfew
DR STEWART JOHNSON

Gambling – A Family Affair
ANGELA WILLANS

Garlic
KAREN EVENNETT

The Good Stress Guide
MARY HARTLEY

Heart Attacks – Prevent and Survive
DR TOM SMITH

**Helping Children Cope with Attention
Deficit Disorder**
DR PATRICIA GILBERT

Helping Children Cope with Bullying
SARAH LAWSON

Helping Children Cope with Divorce
ROSEMARY WELLS

Helping Children Cope with Dyslexia
SALLY RAYMOND

Helping Children Cope with Grief
ROSEMARY WELLS

Hold Your Head Up High
DR PAUL HAUCK

How to Be Your Own Best Friend
DR PAUL HAUCK

How to Cope When the Going Gets Tough
DR WINDY DRYDEN AND JACK
GORDON

How to Cope with Anaemia
DR JOAN GOMEZ

How to Cope with Bulimia
DR JOAN GOMEZ

How to Cope with Difficult Parents
DR WINDY DRYDEN AND JACK
GORDON

How to Cope with Difficult People
ALAN HOUEL WITH CHRISTIAN
GODEFROY

**How to Cope with People who Drive You
Crazy**
DR PAUL HAUCK

How to Cope with Splitting Up
VERA PEIFFER

How to Cope with Stress
DR PETER TYRER

How to Enjoy Your Retirement
VICKY MAUD

How to Improve Your Confidence
DR KENNETH HAMBLY

How to Interview and Be Interviewed
MICHELE BROWN AND GYLES
BRANDRETH

How to Keep Your Cholesterol in Check
DR ROBERT POVEY

How to Love and Be Loved
DR PAUL HAUCK

How to Pass Your Driving Test
DONALD RIDLAND

How to Stand Up for Yourself
DR PAUL HAUCK

**How to Start a Conversation and Make
Friends**
DON GABOR

How to Stick to a Diet
DEBORAH STEINBERG AND
DR WINDY DRYDEN

How to Stop Worrying
DR FRANK TALLIS

How to Untangle Your Emotional Knots
DR WINDY DRYDEN AND JACK
GORDON

How to Write a Successful CV
JOANNA GUTMANN

Overcoming Common Problems Series

Hysterectomy
SUZIE HAYMAN

The Incredible Sulk
DR WINDY DRYDEN

The Irritable Bowel Diet Book
ROSEMARY NICOL

The Irritable Bowel Stress Book
ROSEMARY NICOL

Is HRT Right for You?
DR ANNE MACGREGOR

Jealousy
DR PAUL HAUCK

Learning to Live with Multiple Sclerosis
DR ROBERT POVEY, ROBIN DOWIE
AND GILLIAN PRETT

Living with Angina
DR TOM SMITH

Living with Asthma
DR ROBERT YOUNGSON

Living with Diabetes
DR JOAN GOMEZ

Living with Grief
DR TONY LAKE

Living with High Blood Pressure
DR TOM SMITH

Living with a Stoma
DR CRAIG WHITE

Making the Most of Yourself
GILL FOX AND SHEILA DAINOW

Menopause
RAEWYN MACKENZIE

The Migraine Diet Book
SUE DYSON

Motor Neurone Disease – A Family Affair
DR DAVID OLIVER

The Nervous Person's Companion
DR KENNETH HAMBLY

Out of Work – A Family Affair
ANNE LOVELL

Overcoming Anger
DR WINDY DRYDEN

Overcoming Shame
DR WINDY DRYDEN

Overcoming Stress
DR VERNON COLEMAN

The Parkinson's Disease Handbook
DR RICHARD GODWIN-AUSTEN

The PMS Diet Book
KAREN EVENNETT

Second Time Around
ANNE LOVELL

Serious Mental Illness – A Family Affair
GWEN HOWE

Sex & Relationships
ROSEMARY STONES

The Stress Workbook
JOANNA GUTMANN

The Subfertility Handbook
VIRGINIA IRONSIDE AND SARAH
BIGGS

Talking About Anorexia
How to cope with life without starving
MAROUSHKA MONRO

Ten Steps to Positive Living
DR WINDY DRYDEN

Think Your Way to Happiness
DR WINDY DRYDEN AND JACK
GORDON

**Understanding Obsessions and
Compulsions**
A self-help manual
DR FRANK TALLIS

Understanding Your Personality
Myers-Briggs and more
PATRICIA HEDGES

Overcoming Common Problems

How to Succeed as a
Single Parent

Carole Baldock

sheldon PRESS

First published in Great Britain in 1999 by
Sheldon Press, SPCK, Holy Trinity Church, Marylebone Road, London NW1 4DU

British Library Cataloguing-in-Publication Data
A catalogue for this book is available from the British Library

ISBN 0–85969–805–X

Typeset by Deltatype Ltd, Birkenhead, Merseyside
Printed in Great Britain by
Biddles Ltd, Guildford and King's Lynn

Contents

Part 1 Self

1 Introduction: You Are Not Alone   1
2 Friends, Relations, Neighbours: I   7
3 Friends, Relations, Neighbours: II   11
4 'Ships that Pass in the Night'? The Dating Game   14
5 Health I: Exercise and Eating   17
6 Health II: Problems and Suggestions for Solving
     Them   20

Part 2 Home

7 Form-filling I: Family Credit, Income Support,
     Help with Health Costs, Council Tax, CSA   23
8 Money: Budgeting, Savings and Bills, Debt   31
9 Economizing: Home Repairs and Money-saving
     Tips   35
10 More Money-saving Tips: Food and Shopping   39
11 Life's Little Luxuries: Clothes, Entertainment   42
12 Leisure: Activities, Hobbies and Interests   44

Part 3 Children

13 The After-effects of Divorce   47
14 Childcare   52
15 'We Don't Need No Education'   56
16 Leisure: Children's Activities, Hobbies and
     Interests   59
17 Health Matters   62
18 Teenagers: Sex and Drugs and Rock and Roll   66
19 Holidays   69
20 Money, Money, Money   72
21 Saturday Jobs . . . and Slave Labour   75

Part 4 Work

22 Job or Career: What Are Your Options?   78
23 Self-esteem: Making the Most of Yourself   82
24 Making the Most of Your Skills   85
25 Assessing Your Skills   87
26 Form-filling II: Income Tax, National Insurance,
        Student Grants   91
27 On Course: Further Education   95
28 'We Have the Technology, Now What Do We
        Do with It?' Using Computers when Working
        from Home   98
29 Time-management   101
30 Part-time Work   105
31 Future Prospects   108

    Useful Addresses   113
    Further Reading   123
    Index   129

To Nathan, Cassia and Alysse,
with love and thanks

Part 1 Self

1
Introduction: You Are Not Alone

''Tis better to have married, even if you do end up single, than never to have married at all.' Despite women's lib, women often think they are put on this earth purely to get married and live happily ever after. Even when they give up hope of ever meeting Mr Right, maybe there's a chance of Mr Shed ('Suppose He'll Do'), who is solid and could come in useful. But many women who succeed as single parents find that is what is right for them.

Who Are Single Parents?

Smaller accommodation is currently being built and made available because more people are living on their own, and with the increasing number of single-parent households, it has been predicted that nearly four and a half million new homes will be needed early in the next century. Sixty-five per cent of single parents have been separated, divorced or widowed, with about 6 per cent who intended getting pregnant but not married. Around 5 per cent are career women in their late thirties to early forties, who chose artificial insemination rather than a relationship. Thirty-five per cent of single parents are under 30, less than 5 per cent under 20. Teenage girls who are single parents tend to regard motherhood as prestigious, and had expected to be in a relationship, with over three-quarters claiming their boyfriend wanted a baby.

Little research has been carried out about young single fathers. Many seem proud of their status and aim to do better than their own fathers, but feel excluded from the usual support groups; obstacles like lack of money, home and jobs lead to difficulties about access. Unmarried fathers effectively have no rights, even if their name is on the birth certificate or they pay maintenance. However, often influenced by their own family, particularly the mother, they help

1

out with accommodation and money or buying gifts for the child, such as clothing.

The expression 'single mother' may conjure up the image of a feckless, reckless girl who won't get off her backside to do a decent day's work. It is commonly believed that teenagers deliberately get pregnant to jump housing queues. The first time I heard this notion was in a lecture by a community education teacher to a room full of students of all ages, from all walks of life, and the entire class burst out laughing at the idea. In fact, single parents are usually offered smaller properties than two-parent families, and mother and child are often required to share a bedroom.

The majority of single parents are ordinary women, with enough to cope with, let alone the negativity projected by society in general and the media in particular. Divorce is rarely undertaken without a great deal of thought, and the most frightening thing about it is thinking you'll be on your own. But you are not alone. Here comes the technical bit, so . . . concentrate.

Some Facts and Figures: Divorce

At one in two marriages failing, the UK has the highest divorce rate in Europe, though 70 per cent of Swedish families are headed by single parents. The number of divorces has quadrupled in the past 30 years, with the USA one of the few Western countries whose divorce rate is higher, and one American professor has devised a 15-minute test to predict whether a marriage will last. Only 50 per cent of those wed in the UK in 1994 will celebrate their twenty-fifth anniversary, with the average marriage lasting nine years. Four in ten regard marriage as the ultimate commitment, but for 50 per cent, it is not as important as it used to be. Eleven per cent are put off, because of the divorce rate. Over-45s favour traditional families; under-30s prefer alternative lifestyles, for example, people sharing a household. One quarter of women aged 18 to 49 cohabit, but cohabitation usually breaks up after about two years. A single parent is in a situation which lasts longer, that is, until the children grow up; or until there's another partner, though this is becoming less popular.

More Facts and Figures: Single-parent Families

The total of single-parent families in the UK is approximately 1.7 million; other terms used are 'one-' or 'lone-parent' families, but 'lone' gives an extremely negative impression and rarely appears to be used by parents themselves. In 1996, 36 per cent of babies were born to unmarried parents. Half the single-parent families have one child, about one-third have two (few have large families); comprising about 22 per cent of all children (between 2.4 and 3 million). Some 10 per cent of single parents are fathers, while just over four in ten Black families are headed by a single parent. The dwindling number of 'shotgun marriages', from which there was a high divorce rate, has affected the figures, as the women now tend to remain single instead, and one in five of them has never lived with a partner. However, terminations account for one in five pregnancies (one in two for teenagers) and 80 per cent of abortions are outside marriage.

Facts and Figures: Money

Forty-one per cent of single-parent families have a weekly income under £100, compared with 4 per cent of two-parent families. Of the 65 per cent of people who earn more than £350 per week, only 12 per cent are lone parents. Despite the Child Support Agency (CSA), only about 20 per cent receive maintenance, less than one-tenth of their income. Of the 35 per cent of fathers who never lived with the mother, one-third pay nothing towards the child's upkeep, compared with 10 per cent of divorced fathers. It is claimed that regular payment of maintenance encourages single parents to get jobs. Compared with France (82 per cent) and the USA (60 per cent), the UK has one of the lowest employment rates for single parents: 40 per cent of mothers (compared with 65 per cent of married mothers). So 1.1 million (over 70 per cent) with 1.9 million children rely on Income Support, while 330,000 (with 540,000 children) claim Family Credit; most prefer the latter, even though they may still experience hardship. Seventy-seven per cent of single parents want a job but are thwarted by the lack of affordable childcare, plus the 'benefits trap' when additional costs, such as fares, reduce income to below state benefits level. Around three in ten work full-time or are looking for a job or plan to look for a job in the future. One in ten do not find work.

Over 70 per cent of divorces are initiated by women, and single-parent families may be regarded as one of the results of women's lib. In 1975, one-third of all divorces cited adultery; by 1994, it was down to a quarter, nearly twice as many men (37 per cent) as women

(22 per cent). On average, one in ten husbands have had an affair in the past five years and one in 20 wives; one in eight upper-class men compared with one in 40 manual workers, possibly through having more opportunities. Mothers are less likely to have affairs; having children does not seem to act as a deterrent on men. But over three-quarters of married men (80 per cent) and women (86 per cent) more or less agree that sex outside marriage is mostly wrong.

Useful Organizations

The National Council for One Parent Families (NCOPF), set up in 1918 as the National Council for the Unmarried Mother and her Child, to rescue them from starvation on the streets, 'works to enable lone parents to create and sustain a secure and rewarding life for themselves and their children'. In 1970, the support group, Gingerbread, was established when social services would not help Raga Woods unless her family had nowhere to go. The name is said to come from a café which provided her with refreshments on the house.

Cruse – Bereavement Care is the largest organization of its kind in the world, established in 1959 by Margaret Torrie, following an immediate response when she placed an advert about forming a group for young widows. The title comes from an Old Testament story about a widow who shared her last jar of oil (cruse) with a stranger, the Hebrew prophet, Elijah. It was chosen to emphasize the idea of support and encouragement, especially since 'widowed' comes from the French *vide*, meaning empty. The service has officially included widowers since 1980, and is now a registered charity with about 200 branches throughout the UK.

Bereavement

When becoming a single parent is the result of bereavement, there is support from those around you as well as people outside your immediate circle, that is, officialdom. You receive a great deal of advice, some of it conflicting, but finally it is down to you, and this is where the bond between you and your children should grow stronger. However, sometimes, the bereaved partner receives all the help and support, particularly when children are grown up, instead of mutual comfort from parent to children and vice versa being provided. With younger children, the initial instinct is to protect them as much as possible, even to the extent of not being wholly honest. Telling them that the other parent has gone away or is in hospital can be a dangerous way of postponing the moment of truth.

A death in the family makes children frightened about losing the surviving parent, and no matter how painful it is to discuss, they should be allowed to talk about what has happened in order to alleviate their fears. According to some reports, nearly half of them may end up taking drugs (one in five where they have lost both parents); drugs and pregnancy are more common with 18-year-old girls when a parent has died rather than when parents separate. Arrangements can be made for you to talk to a counsellor, something which may also benefit the children. For example, it can be difficult to come to a decision about children visiting the chapel of rest or attending the funeral; many people hold such strong views about paying their respects/sparing the children that it causes considerable disruption in families.

Try to ensure that life gets back to normal; let the children invite friends round or go out, even though you want a bit of peace or somebody to keep you company. Don't discourage them from talking about the deceased parent because keeping their memory alive comforts you all; one suggestion is to work together making a journal or a scrapbook. Include your children in making plans about the future and always provide reassurance about how much you love them.

Single Parents: Pros and Cons?

Single parents are still sometimes thought of as selfish adults who put their own interests ahead of those of their children, and they may be stigmatized as unwilling to seek work when they can claim social security benefits. However, single parenthood is starting to be seen as a stage in the family life cycle, instead of automatically being regarded as either second rate or imperfect, that is, differing from the norm. The tide may have begun to turn with the protests about Labour's decision to cut benefits (though Harriet Harman thought 90 per cent of single mothers want to earn money). This made even worse one of the harshest of Catch-22 situations: women from an impoverished background often end up as single parents, and women who become single parents end up struggling for money.

Their main problems are social and economic. They may experience poverty and they have to learn to cope with total responsibility, loneliness and guilt (obligation to others). There are also many positive aspects: peaceful atmosphere, contentment, independence, resilience. Priorities are: children's well-being, a satisfying job, decent housing, good health, reliable childcare. Along with the insistence on getting single parents to work, there is equally pressure on them to stay at home when they have young children, because they are single parents. The argument here is that children have greater need of them since their upbringing cannot be shared with a partner. It is also important that children have regular contact with other adults who will also act as role models, for example, in childcare, although parents who have not had recourse to it are not always convinced that it's a good idea.

Society nowadays breeds 'wannabes': 'I want it, and I want it now', though if you usually make do with custard creams, you enjoy chocolate biscuits all the more. Delayed gratification is almost a forgotten concept, except where women are concerned. They are expected to be mother, wife, daughter, and are invariably regarded as selfish if they ever dream of putting themselves first. Is this why so many girls yearn for marriage, so sure nothing else will guarantee their happiness? But a women who isn't at peace with herself and largely content with her life can't expect somebody else to make her happy. Nor is it possible for her to make others happy, including her children.

2

Friends, Relations, Neighbours: I

Divorce is one of the scariest situations anyone has to face. A whole new ball game, and you can't seem to get the hang of the rules, especially concerning your relationships with others. Opinions are mixed, ranging from 'Good for you!' to 'But how will you ever manage? What'll happen to the children?' (well, I *was* thinking of borrowing a she-wolf from the zoo; it worked well in Rome, so I understand). You have to cope with a rapid change in status, and not only where money is concerned. For those in their fifties and sixties, divorce is still regarded as shameful, nor are they used to handling finances because 'my husband dealt with all that sort of thing'. Women in their thirties and forties are usually more independent, but have young children to worry about.

The Single Parent in Society, at Home

The ideal situation in which to raise 2.4 children (boy, girl and one on the way, presumably) is a couple who love and respect each other. It comes as a shock to discover that society firmly believes that it is far better for children to be brought up in the worst of so-called nuclear families than in the best of single-parent families. An even bigger shock is to find that's what many of your family and friends feel. Most of us aren't particularly bothered about what the government or the media are currently shaking their head over, but we do expect a degree of understanding from those closest to us.

Prepare yourself: for years after the divorce, bump into anyone you know and the very first question is always whether you've met somebody new. Then they remember their manners and ask after the children. Don't wait to be asked. Tell them you're doing fine, casually reeling off examples. Positive thinking boosts your self-esteem, and it means that one day you won't wake up flooded with astonishment that you (you, of all people!) are divorced. This, incidentally, usually precedes great regret that you have a wardrobe full of clothes and no chance of wearing any of them ever again. You will. And you'll be buying more.

Astonishment is the usual reaction to news of divorce, and yours in particular, and you may be pressurized to reconsider, regardless of the circumstances. All good things must come to an end, and even when it is blatantly obvious that the marriage has not been a good thing for some time, your nearest and dearest will move heaven and earth to persuade you not to rock the boat. At times like this, no cliché is left unturned. And no stone. Everyone gets slapped in the face with dirty laundry.

Friends

You can choose your friends but you can't choose your family. A friend in need is a friend indeed, or a flaming nuisance. You now have some idea of the truth of these statements, dismayed to find you cannot always depend on those you believed to be reliable, yet experiencing kindness from unexpected quarters. You'll be touched to realize just how many friends you have, though distressed when some of them simply accept the situation, regardless of right or wrong, and quicker than you can say '*La femme est morte. Vive la femme!*'

There are your friends and his friends, and then your joint friends; in the end, who really was the villain of the piece does not appear to count for much.

- Some will take sides
- Some will strive to remain neutral
- Some will meddle and make matters even more complicated.

Having been rejected by the one who was supposed to love you most of all, now others are doing the same, because they've accepted The Other Person. It's hard not to feel betrayed, and becomes even more agonizing when your children show signs of liking Them. Once life starts getting back to normal, most people believe in civilized behaviour, no matter if it seems hypocritical. That's the way of the world and, in time, you learn to accept it.

Friendship comes in many shapes and forms, from bestest friends with no time for anyone else, to people with loads of acquaintances, including a few they are close to. Some always stay friends with those from primary school, others have the knack of making friends easily but don't make the effort to maintain the relationship. Most of us have friends in different spheres – home, work, school, leisure – not all of whom necessarily get on with one another, as you discover the first time you throw a party.

Reformed junkies often claim they only recovered by moving away from their usual friends. That's one extreme, but if you stay in the same circle as your Ex, there'll be more problems than if you move on and make new friends. Remember, though, you cannot expect to like everybody you meet, nor can you expect everyone to like you. Again, that's the way it is; don't take it personally or as proof of the stigma of being a single parent.

Friendly Advice

Professionals are often in a better position than your friends to offer comfort, support and practical advice – doctors, counsellors, people at your place of work, teaching staff at your children's school(s); regular churchgoers should be able to rely on other members rallying round.

Stress often manifests as physical symptoms, and people who know their doctor well are able to confide in them. Those of us who dislike anything reminiscent of hospital, or feel that we shouldn't take up Doctor's valuable time, can always jot down a couple of urgent problems; two less worries should make life easier. When psychotherapy or counselling is recommended, even if sceptical, give it a try. It takes a long time to get everything out of your system, and these methods help you come to terms with it. Besides, hearing the same things over and over again wears away at your friends' sympathy. Eventually, you have to let go, deal with what's happened, and move on. It's far easier when you are being offered gentle encouragement, than feeling forced into it because everybody's fed up with your one topic of conversation.

Friendly Gatherings

Clubs and societies are not everyone's cup of tea (or large glass of cheap wine), but it helps to know you're not on your own, easing you into a new way of life, when you're out of the habit of socializing. Look on it as a means to an end, not an end in itself, and a new audience, providing you return the favour by being a good listener. This gives you a sense of perspective, and revives your sense of (black) humour. No matter how badly done to you feel, you'll hear plenty of tales of the unexpected: the husband whose wife sailed off as they were awaiting his boss for a dinner party; the wife whose husband slept with his daughter-in-law-to-be the night before their son's wedding.

At work, explain about your situation, since the effects have probably not passed unnoticed; sympathy is more readily forthcoming than if you inexplicably become unreliable and over-emotional. There should be somebody you can pour your heart out to. If it's hard to cope, you'll need time off, although some people bury themselves in their work to help to get them through. Sticking to a regular routine makes you more confident about being able to get your life back into some kind of order.

Similarly, let the school know what's happened. One recent report suggests that no good will come of this, and pupils may be penalized since their new status means lower expectations on the part of the teachers. As this emanates from the USA, it may have little bearing on UK schools. In the UK, there are some areas where classes are virtually divided between children from single-parent and two-parent families. If you've been involved with your children's schooling and know their teachers reasonably well, you'll find most of them have their pupils' welfare at heart. They will do their best for them in difficult circumstances, and make allowances.

3

Friends, Relations, Neighbours: II

Keeping it in the Family

Family life is the result of patterns and traditions, but our experience differs from our mother's more than hers did from her mother's. Most women claim to be happier than their mothers, though working women have less contact, with fewer than 50 per cent seeing their mothers once a week. Those who do have dropped from 64 per cent to 45 per cent in the past ten years. Studies in the 1950s and 1960s showed that the strongest link was between mothers and daughters, keeping wider families together. Society, especially the media and the government, upholds an image of two-parent families cemented in the 1950s, with Victorian undertones. And though we can be trained – through education, career, raising children and self-development – marriage is left mostly to chance and intuition.

Being hard up is not necessarily a disadvantage when it comes to divorce. We may admire people who stick together 'for the sake of the children', but few voice their fears of losing big cars, beautiful homes and holidays abroad. Some couples stay married from habit, accustomed to a certain standard of living. Many older women put up with a great deal rather than face an uncertain future; better the devil you know . . . Younger women have less to lose, and it is suggested they marry knowing they can get divorced if it doesn't work. We often have to choose between security (risking boredom) or freedom (plain risky), and fortunately are usually resilient enough to cope with change; if we cannot adapt, we do not develop.

Divorce is unique to each person, according to their way of life, where they live, how they live. People with a good family life are at a loss to understand those who have never had that pleasure, even if it's true of the person they marry. Although middle-aged women don't always get on with their parents (or their mother), women in their twenties and thirties often enjoy better relationships, receiving more sympathy and support.

However, even in the 1970s, divorce in the family was regarded with horror. Now, women with three children are reassured that 'it was bound to happen', but it still scandalizes the older generation. It is not just the middle classes. Mothers from all classes are appalled about what the neighbours will think, because it reflects badly on them: 'I didn't bring you up to treat people like that' or 'I didn't bring you up to be treated like that'. More trouble arises if your family can't understand why you have anything more to do with your Ex's family, and when it is suspected that loyalty is not 100 per cent although the 'peace-makers' are probably trying to view both sides of the situation.

The relationship of each parent with each child is affected by that parent's position in their own family when they were a child. A parent who was an only child is appalled by the ferocity of fights between siblings, and perplexed by their equally ferocious loyalty. Conversely, a parent from a large family worries about the only child who prefers their own company. The two main personality types – introvert and extrovert – also make a difference. With divorce, the former risks becoming totally introspective, while the latter has to be the life and soul of the party. Taken to extremes, both are dangerous courses of action.

Neighbours

In the good old days, community spirit reigned, allegedly; front and back doors were left unlocked, and a night out left you with change from a £1 note. Nowadays, whether we live in town or country, street or estate, few of us know much about our neighbours. Families with children of a similar age are more likely to develop a relationship beyond the occasional 'good morning', although not necessarily one you can automatically rely on. Single mothers are sometimes regarded with great suspicion by married women, and with envy by unhappily married women.

When two sets of children are close friends, it's worth staying on good terms with other parents, but you may suddenly become better acquainted with your neighbours because of the gossip. Most of us enjoy a good natter, but some relish scandal and start taking an interest to discover exactly what's going on. Friendships can start off under odd circumstances, but though it may be easier to unburden yourself to a comparative stranger, not everybody will keep confidences.

Problems and Solutions

In your unexpectedly acquired state of independence, what do you do when disaster strikes? Members of what is delicately described as 'the silver market' invariably declare that they've never been dependent on charity, and they're not going to start now. Fine words butter no parsnips nor ensure a basic diet, unless you're prepared to swallow your pride (thoroughly mixing metaphors). It's bad enough being hard up and labelled a scrounger, but there are times when you have to ask for help. You may need somebody to keep an eye on the baby while you nip out for milk, or to find someone with an idea why the blasted washing machine won't empty.

You can either agonize whenever something goes wrong or you can rationalize. What if it were the other way round? What if my neighbour needed help from me? Few people resent helping out and 'do unto others' is fairly universal, though some have no qualms about borrowing anything (including money), demanding help from others as their basic right instead of making any effort to help themselves. Most of us aren't like that, and people don't imagine that we are, single parent or not. Besides, there will be opportunities to return a favour: picking up a prescription or posting a letter. Doing somebody a good turn makes you feel better, and shows you that there really are people far worse off than you.

At some point you'll realize that, with a little help from those around you, you can cope, and life goes on, perhaps to bigger and better things. This is a revelation, which can hit you whether you are consoling the children after burying their pet rabbit, or having a very late-night expensive supper in a café bar, or taking photographs of your daughter in Bond Street.

4

'Ships that Pass in the Night'?
The Dating Game

Going on a date takes getting used to, particularly if you were married a long time (and your husband was your first boyfriend – naming no names). Maybe you feel it's better to have a close encounter of any kind, rather than a quick drink with Mr Shed? Or, at the other extreme, you've had more dates than a Christmas hamper? It's a jungle out there, and if your machete has gone rusty, it can be extremely nerve-racking. What do I wear? Where do I go? Who will I meet? How do I know if he *really* likes me?

Introductions all round

What will my family and friends think of him? And what will the children think? One thing's for sure, they don't want somebody to take the place of their dad. Unfortunately, Mr Shed is likely to assume this is his role. Or he'll be one of those idiots who think kids want parents to be their friends (which they do, but not all the time). However, no matter how much you love your children, they will probably be gradually introduced into the conversation, so Mr Shed can get used to the idea of their existence. Being a grown man, this doesn't take as long (in theory) as it does with the children, although neither always take kindly to it. Fortunately, offspring have rather more resilience and common sense than they are sometimes given credit for, probably because adults think they know best. Reassured of their place in your affections, children generally learn to adapt to most situations.

'Nuclear families' – though an appropriate phrase since many of them end up blown apart – are no longer common, and family units are said to be dwindling because relatives no longer tend to live within popping-in distance. In fact, many families have grown, sprawling through a confusing range of step-relatives. Blood may be thicker than water, but watered-down relationships can be harmonious, although some suspect that the wicked stepmother (and any other step-) is not a myth.

Even if you are a divorcée who initially chooses to 'get thee to a nunnery', you may later decide to enter the dating arena, though by then your children are used to having you all to themselves. If they're reluctant to share you with siblings, Mr Shed stands little chance, so once he's a speck on the horizon, lay the groundwork by discussing the situation with them. This isn't necessarily any business of family and friends, and don't start imagining that everyone is eagle-eyeing you because, well, we *all* know you've failed once, so what makes you think you can make a success of any relationship? Thoughts of that nature mean it's doomed to fail, crashing on the rocks of desperation.

Whoever you go out with is your children's business because what affects you will affect them, and you'll need patience and common sense to deal with the situation, without succumbing to guilt. Going out for the evening doesn't mean you are shamefully neglecting the children, though it's easy to allow such thoughts to hijack your brain, especially when arranging a babysitter. Not all grandparents vie for the privilege; even when married, you may have had to flip a coin (and if you lost, you rang *his* mother: just-this-once-if-you-possibly-could-because-well-it-is-his-birthday-after-all).

Friends again

There are some advantages with major traumas, the main one being that you don't know your own strength. With divorce, the other is knowing who your real friends are. Hang on to them: good friends are good friends, right or wrong, good or bad. Do your best not to neglect them but don't let it spoil things if you feel they're neglecting you. Good friendship will survive a bad row, and in these busy, busy times, a certain amount of juggling is called for. When women fall in love, friends tend to be shunted to the back of the queue; alas, two best friends in the company of a halfway decent bloke are often transformed into rivals, consciously or unconsciously.

Post divorce, whether painting the town red or sitting at home with the blues, keep in contact. When you're ready to socialize/calm down, you could make a start by arranging a get-together with your closest friends, going for a meal or a few drinks, visiting the cinema or the theatre. If, as a result, Mr Shed looms up, all well and good.

Hi, Societies

You could ginger up your social life by joining a group, from cookery classes to dating agencies. Courses in car maintenance or computers used to be recommended (a little knowledge can be a very useful thing to avoid huge bills) but *haute cuisine* is currently hot. Dating agencies have a curious mix of risk and stigma attached to them; friendship and correspondence clubs may be more suitable, and the ground rules applied to the former come in useful.

- *Do* arrange to meet for the first time in a public place (bars or restaurants), preferably one you already know.
- *Do* keep your family and friends fully informed about it (the meeting, not Mr Shed).
- *Don't* give your address or agree for the first meeting to be 'your place or mine?'
- *Don't* accept a lift or arrange to meet again if you have any doubts whatsoever.

You are not being paranoid by insisting on a few simple rules, and should not be made to feel uncomfortable about it. Trust your instincts. And that also applies when dealing with family, friends and children.

5

Health I: Exercise and Eating

As civilization knocks up nearly two thousand years, we can choose from the latest in technology or delve into old wives' tales from both East and West. Never before have we been so conscious of what good health entails – nor of how many things can go wrong with the human body. On offer is a staggering array, so start investigating until content that you've found what suits you. Single parents need to keep themselves as fit and well as possible, for their own sake and for their children's. You can enrol at a health centre with all kinds of sophisticated gym equipment on offer ('state-of-the-art' meaning you soon get into a state, figuring out how the flaming thing works) or work out a set of exercises to do at home. Choice of food has never been greater; one chef regards his main challenge to be creating dishes unlikely to be found in a supermarket ready-meal range.

Gym'll fix it

Nevertheless, we are not a super-fit nation; more people are officially classified as obese which, unfortunately, also applies to children. Ironically, the bad old days with more hard work and more walking helped keep the calories in their place. Now, we need scarcely move to get what we want, unless it's to clamber into the car.

Exercise has its fans and its foes but there's plenty of choice, and it's worth experimenting to find something stimulating. Extroverts aim for team games or sports involving a social life; introverts may need their own space but can emerge occasionally to mix with people. For extroverts, to be alone means loneliness, but the odd half-hour does as much good as a bit of socializing does an introvert. Sport can be exhilarating, and even if not particularly skilful, you usually have a good laugh. If you unearth an unsuspected talent, it does wonders for you.

Having worked your way through the gamut (from aikido to, well, there must be something beginning with 'z' by now), if nothing suits, 20 minutes spent working out, three times a week, should keep

17

you healthy. You may loathe it, but habits become more bearable because of the sense of relief once you've finished (plus the days you don't have to exercise). Self-discipline is often underrated but – no pain, no gain.

Food, Glorious Food

Self-discipline also plays a part in beating those villains of eating disorders: anorexia or bulimia. Although it is accepted that these are psychological problems, people who are fat are condemned as just plain greedy, though this, too, is likely to have a psychological basis rather than stemming from well-known genes. And the most effective way to lose weight is not chasing after the latest dieting bandwagon, but to eat less and exercise more, which also helps the pounds stay off. However, no matter how strongly you feel, you may refuse to buy food which is less fat or low calorie (whoever imagined that 'lite' has a persuasive ring to it?). If your weight starts increasing, something needs to be done about it, preferably before you give up the struggle to get into your favourite jeans. Ideal weight? As long as your knickers fit properly, why torture yourself?

Figuring it out

Parents are expected to set standards for their children to follow but single parents don't have someone to back them up or provide a balance by quietly pointing out alternatives. Most parents are terrified at the idea of predicaments like eating disorders, and though losing weight to suit yourself is one thing, if you are obsessive about food it will have a detrimental effect on your offspring. Yet, considering the horrific mealtime scenes parents undergo with toddlers, it's a wonder every child doesn't grow up with problems.

And surely few adults are influenced by the media when it comes to possessing a willowy figure? They may envy some celebrities but are rarely hell-bent on achieving exactly the same shape. Insisting that teenage girls are always dieting to emulate their role models seems odd, when they're more likely to be affected by peer pressure. The Holy Grail of a perfect shape? We are all individuals, all different shapes and sizes, and need to find out what suits us best. Each of us has a particular metabolism. For example, some people eat like a horse and never put on an ounce, whereas others reckon one quick glance at a cream cake adds a pound. Fruit and vegetables are usually fairly cheap, though some of us simply couldn't face the recommended five daily portions and augment it with fruit juice, yoghurt, fromage frais and so on.

Reading about food is bewildering, with so much information, and so many contradictions. How often does flavour of the month become not-to-be-touched-with-a-barge-pole? If you feel comfortable with your doctor, ask their advice and they will arrange a programme for you best suited to your needs, including being weighed at regular intervals. Bathroom scales have a lot to answer for, and there's no question that the best thing to do is chuck them out.

6

Health II: Problems and Suggestions for Solving Them

Stress and Anxiety

Stress is pandemic these days; it's the twentieth-century disease. Despite all the mod cons and the general increase in standards of living, we always find something to worry about. In small, manageable doses, stress does some good, galvanizing us into making one last supreme effort to win at sport or gain top marks in an exam. Once out of control, it rapidly becomes overwhelming. Panic attacks are a horrifying experience; anyone fortunate enough never to have been in such a 'life-or-death' situation will have a vague idea if they recall how they felt waiting to take their driving test or to sit a vital exam.

Virtually everyone comes under stress, at work, at home or even play, and it swiftly infiltrates everywhere. Parents may sometimes literally worry themselves sick, particularly in families where both have jobs; work is usually more stressful than home, since it is less under your control. Even the most resourceful woman must juggle marriage, career and children; it's implicit that the last two inevitably contend for second place. Most women expect some help and support from their partner but find that the old man never has been and never will be a 'new man'. If it turns out that he is basically another kid to look after, then a single parent is, effectively, under less stress.

But what about companionship? Marriage is no guarantee of good company. They say the worst loneliness is when you're in a crowd, but it must be unbearable living with somebody who is out most of the time, and has next to nothing to say when they're at home. Men are not exactly known for in-depth, emotional conversation at the best of times, let alone when they can't be bothered to communicate at all.

Depression

Depression is as painful as anxiety but while the latter can be triggered by an actual incident, experts still argue over the cause of the former. It also may be externally caused, or internal, due to something psychological or some form of chemical imbalance, when it can be cured by drugs or by psychoanalysis. Depression needs prompt attention because it can be catching; living with depressed parents may cause the same condition in children, and it is on record that some as young as four have depression. Furthermore, it is cursed with chicken-and-egg syndrome; is it psychosomatic, resulting in physical malfunction, or does this cause the depression? Hence the saying: 'healthy mind, healthy body'. Having to put up with a variety of symptoms (if not all at the same time) – headache, sleeplessness, eczema, hair loss, splitting nails, weight gain or loss – is difficult even when you feel fine in yourself. If, on top of that little lot, you are depressed, life as a whole becomes intolerable.

Possible Solutions

There are many remedies, however, some of which will work for you. Counselling may be derided, but many people benefit from literally talking something out of their system, though for some, their condition will worsen if they are allowed to dwell too much on the subject. Others recover with medication while some are capable of sorting it out for themselves, which is like an insurance policy. Knowing you've conquered depression through your own efforts gives you confidence to be able to cope, should it return.

If you've ever fallen out with somebody close to you and didn't patch it up immediately, you know how it gets harder with each passing day to try to improve the situation. It's the same with stress-related illnesses. Single parents may have gone through a divorce, which also involves money problems, possibly the loss of a job or having to move house. The odds are stacked up against them, and that takes its toll. It's said that people don't commit suicide because of depression as such but they do at the point when it starts to lift; up until that time, they are too down to do anything. That's why it's important to seek help as soon as possible, although this involves taking action, which is far from easy even in the early stages. Talking to somebody is a comfort; rely on your doctor as well as your friends.

A more manageable method may be reading up on the subject. In theory, finding out about others suffering from depression and anxiety enables you to put your own problems into perspective, but it may make you more depressed. Once you can read about it, or write about it, quite dispassionately, it's a good indication that you've won this battle. Distraction displaces depression, at least temporarily, and one solution is to find some activity, no matter what, be it jigsaws or playing football, which keeps you sufficiently preoccupied. Above all, remember that if it is the brain which activates depression and anxiety, there's no reason why the brain can't put a stop to them. And they don't last for ever. You will get over them.

Part 2 Home

7

Form-filling I: Family Credit, Income Support, Help with Health Costs, Council Tax, CSA

Help with Disentangling Red Tape

A necessary evil? When it comes to 'the devil finds work for idle hands', it's clear that said hands are in the employ of officialdom. One look at the contents of those dreaded brown envelopes fills everyone with horror, but there are people who understand these things and can help you to complete them:

- The local library.
- The local community centre, especially if English is not your first language.
- The Citizens Advice Bureau. Check opening times; lack of funding and volunteers means they may be open only a few hours each week, and consequently are very busy.
- Social Services Freeline: 0800 666555. Have a cushion ready because they can take ages to reply. Avoid Monday mornings – in fact, first thing every morning, when they're busiest; conversely, Friday afternoons can be too slack to get things done.

Social services may arrange an interview in their department to help you complete their forms. This will probably involve another long wait, so take a picnic and a copy of *War and Peace*. Write out first what you need to know, and bring a pen and notebook to jot down information. Make a copy of the forms for future reference. Some forms crop up regularly (see also Part 4), while others vary. For example, a council grant can take years to sort out – six, in my case, following an application to pay for repairs to prevent the kitchen floor sliding inexorably downwards.

- Mortgage – transfer of interest (don't panic if the building society sends the wrong standard letter, blithely informing you that the house is being sold; as far as they're concerned, it's a similar procedure).
- Life assurance – it's a comfort to know that, on paper at least, financially, you are better off dead.
- Pension – usually arranged after remarks on the lines of, 'Well, you're not getting any younger, you know.'

Social Services

Having to deal with two of their offices, or two in the council, is particularly annoying, and you soon become convinced that the left hand hasn't even noticed there is such a thing as a right hand. For example, a self-employed single parent with teenage children needs to fill in forms to do with all the following:

- Family Credit
- Council Tax Benefit
- Income Tax returns
- Student grant applications.

Being organized makes dealing with paperwork easier. Label a large brown envelope in huge capital letters and put it in a safe place, to keep the most frequently requested documents together:

- Birth certificates
- National Insurance numbers
- Divorce papers
- Pension documents
- Mortgage details
- Tax assessment
- Details of income (expenditure as well as payments).

People who work from 9 a.m. to 5 p.m. on a regular salary find it hard to believe that others can manage (just about) on an extremely low income. The Benefits Agency (Family Credit) and the Education Department are generally helpful, but be prepared for officials who are convinced you're pulling a fast one. It doesn't happen often, but forms should always be carefully completed. Other officials allow for mistakes, even remarkably foolish things like submitting Income Tax returns showing the wrong dates; to err is human, to be forgiven is a huge relief.

Family Credit

Along with the monthly payments, a notification of remission is provided for claiming travelling expenses if you have to go to hospital, or accompany your children while they have treatment. Other benefits include:

- Free prescriptions
- Free dental treatment and dentures
- Vouchers towards the cost of glasses
- Free wigs and fabric supports.

If you receive Family Credit, your children are not entitled to free school meals, as they come in the Income Support payments, but you may receive help with childcare costs up to the September following the child's eleventh birthday; for a registered childminder, nursery or playscheme, nursery or playscheme on government property, or an out-of-hours club (run by the school or the local authority). The four-page form mainly concerns details of the costs incurred, and includes a declaration to be signed by the childminder or nursery manager.

Family Credit is made up of three basic elements:

- An amount for you and your partner, if you have one
- An amount for each child, according to age, until they reach 19
- An amount if you work 30 hours or more a week.

Figures increase slightly each year, varying according to the number and age of your children, as well as your earnings. For example, in 1998, maximum Family Credit for a parent earning less than £77.15 a week with one dependent child was £83 per week.

Are You Entitled to Family Credit?

As Family Credit is a social security benefit providing a regular tax-free cash payment for working people (including the self-employed) with children, the following conditions apply:

- You are a resident in the UK
- You or your partner work at least 16 hours a week
- You or your partner support at least one child who normally lives with you
- You do not have savings of £8,000 or more between you.

Family Credit is not a loan; you don't have to pay it back. It lasts for 26 weeks and is not affected by any change in circumstances during that time. For example, if maintenance ceases because your ex-husband has suddenly gone on the dole, it doesn't go up; if your daughter drops out of school and runs off to get married, it doesn't go down.

When you first apply, there is a 'fast service' so your claim can be dealt with more quickly. If newly employed, or self-employed, you don't have to wait until you receive any wages, as payment can be based on estimated earnings.

How to Apply

Claim form FC1 should be completed with all relevant information, answer boxes ticked, contact numbers provided where possible (daytime or evening), the declaration signed and dated. Send all the required documentary evidence in the prepaid envelope provided:

- Birth certificates
- Pension documents
- Payslips and accounts
- Savings details.

If you are self-employed, complete form FCS501 as well, giving details of income and expenses, unless submitting accounts. You will receive a letter of acknowledgement, and once your claim has been settled, a further letter will advise as follows:

- The amount you will receive and how it has been calculated
- Where it will be paid
- How to appeal if you disagree with the decision
- What other help is available
- The notification of remission, which provides proof when you claim help with NHS charges.

Income Support

Many single parents are automatically entitled to Income Support, but savings between £3,000 and £8,000 affect the amount you receive and over £8,000 makes you ineligible. It is also available as a means-tested benefit, for people over 18 who are working less than 16 hours a week, depending on the amount they earn, and can be used to top up part-time earnings. Free school dinners and free milk (or at a reduced cost) for under-fives are provided, and other benefits include applications to the Social Fund for:

- Financial emergencies; loans for essentials and crises
- Help with funeral costs
- Maternity payments
- Cold weather payments.

Help with Health Costs

If you don't receive Income Support or Family Credit, income-based Job Seeker's Allowance or Disability Working Allowance, you may be able to apply for some help under the NHS Low Income Scheme. You can claim for yourself, your partner and/or your children, providing that you (and your partner) do not have more than £8,000 in savings, or £16,000 if you are in a residential care home or nursing home. You can reclaim your money if health costs were paid for before you were getting benefits, providing you do so within three months (other than the sight test for which the time allowed is 14 days). You can get a refund claim form from social security offices or NHS hospitals (AG5/HC5). Help is available for the following:

- NHS prescriptions, dental treatment
- Sight tests, glasses and contact lenses
- NHS wigs and fabric supports
- Travel to hospital for NHS treatment

Leaflet HC11 ('Are you entitled to help with health costs?') is available from post offices, hospitals and social security offices, and some doctors, dentists, opticians and pharmacists. Or ask at the Citizens Advice Bureau or ring the Health Benefits Division: 0191 203 5555 (Prescription Pricing Authority, Sandyford House, Newcastle upon Tyne NE2 1DB).

Form HC1 includes guidelines; the actual application includes all the sections you are already familiar with: personal details, dependants, income, savings, outgoings. A reply normally takes about four weeks. Your claim is assessed in the usual way, that is, income is compared with requirements, but you can appeal against their decision or complain if you are dissatisfied with the way it has been dealt with. Otherwise, you receive a certificate for help with payments; a new HC1 form needs to be completed four weeks before this runs out.

Council Tax and Housing Benefit

If you have a mortgage and you are on Income Support, only the interest will be covered after two months (nine months if the mortgage was taken out after October 1995). Maximum Housing and Council Tax Benefit are paid to Income Support claimants; Housing Benefit, which is means tested, is to help pay rent. Savings must be less than £16,000 and the amount of benefit is dependent on income and the size of the family, and you may be entitled to them due to circumstances or to low income. For example, the Council Tax Benefit can mean a discount of 100 per cent for students, or 25 per cent if one child is a student. Housing Benefit is calculated according to income:

* Earnings
* Child Benefit and One Parent Benefit
* Family Credit
* Maintenance.

What central government considers your requirements are based on:

* Age of children
* Lone parent over 18
* Family premium
* Lone parent premium.

Always double-check these sums *and* get somebody else to look at them as well. When one assessment takes nearly two years of recalculations (finally reduced by £80), you can't be blamed for suspecting there must be a shortage of batteries for calculators and that mental arithmetic is a dying art. If you have any queries, write, keeping a copy of each letter as written proof in the event of problems. If you ring, one result is an increase in your phone bill. The actual form isn't too bad, and helpfully suggests you contact the Housing Benefit Office or take it to the nearest Area Information Office if you need assistance:

1 About you and your partner (names, addresses, etc.)
2 Personal details (married, single, etc.)
3 People who live in the property
4 Money coming in
5 Other information (pension, childcare, etc.).

Relevant documents which need to be submitted:

- Daily records or audited accounts, if you are self-employed. NB: Even if you are entitled to maximum Family Credit, sending a copy of their confirmation letter is not acceptable. A day book or a declaration with details of earnings and expenses has to be submitted.
- Details of student grant, including term dates (that is, a letter of confirmation from the university or college)
- Proof of savings.

It's recommended that you obtain a receipt from the counter clerk, if hand delivering the necessary documents. When posting them, ask for a certificate of posting, which is free from the post office. Any change in circumstance (income, age of children, moving house, etc.) which might affect benefit must be notified immediately by letter.

Dealing with the Child Support Agency (CSA)

'Maintenance' is regular payment made by the absent parent to help towards the cost of looking after their children. Claiming maintenance for yourself has to be done through the courts but child maintenance can be paid directly to you via the CSA or the courts. The calculation takes into account both the circumstances of each individual family and those of the absent parent, and the amount paid will be based on the net incomes of both parents and everyday living expenses, plus housing costs. Where the absent parent is concerned, care of any of their own or adopted children who are living with them (other than stepchildren) will also be taken into consideration.

Men who lose touch with their family are consequently unlikely to continue to pay maintenance; some make no payments at all. The CSA was established as a result of the Child Support Act 1991 to handle maintenance payments for children, whether or not their parents were married, and has come in for much criticism. Cases of incompetence have risen to Kafkaesque levels, with several incidents of suicide. Men who never pay maintenance seem to be left in peace, yet those who have taken on this responsibility and thus are easier to trace may find themselves hounded.

Parents who receive state benefit are legally obliged to provide details of the absent parent in order for the CSA to obtain payment. If you do not cooperate, your benefit will be reduced (by nearly half), as it will be once you start to receive maintenance. Income Support is reduced pound for pound while a proportion of maintenance (currently the first £15) is disregarded when calculating Family Credit. If you are reluctant to comply because you feel you or your children would 'risk undue harm or distress', you must advise the Child Support Officer of your reasons in writing.

8

Money: Budgeting, Savings and Bills, Debt

Trying to Make it all add up

We're not all good at maths, but practice makes perfect and the less money you have, the more time you spend doing sums. Start with a budget plan, and *don't* cheat by leaving anything out or rounding down odd amounts on debits; take care of the pennies or they soon amount to pounds. Calculate your income: wages, benefits or maintenance, maybe some financial support from your family; it may be easier (and more accurate) to split it up: quarterly, monthly and weekly. Expenditure needs a bigger piece of paper:

- Rent or mortgage
- Travel: shopping in town, visiting friends, nights out, work
- Household: food, cleaning materials, toiletries
- Bills: phone, electricity, gas, insurance, TV (licence and rental), credit cards
- Books, magazines, newspapers, CDs, drinks, cigarettes
- Going out: restaurants, clubs, cinema, theatre, concerts, sports
- Clothes
- Any extras, such as presents and holidays.

Deduct outgoings from income to find the balance . . . Well, at least everyone you know is roughly in the same boat, that is, a mess. You also need to try and save some cash; never mind rainy days, problems can flood in. Money often doesn't turn up in time (the legendary cheque in the post), and disasters include having to turn down a good night out through lack of funds.

Learning to Economize

There are two ways to make ends meet: increase income or reduce spending. It takes will-power to learn to be thrifty, but it's worth the effort. Some of us are born with it but enjoy watching savings accumulate so much we can't bear to part with them. Others never seem to hang on to their cash. Most of us fall somewhere in between and can get into the habit of saving. Sticking small change in a jam jar may seem childish (silver rather than coppers, because the bank clerk will hate you on sight as you stagger through the door) but it mounts up. Admittedly £10 a month won't buy a Caribbean cruise but you'll get an evening out. Whenever you cut down on something, such as walking instead of getting the bus, use the money saved for a specific purpose rather than squander it.

Once you've enough to open a savings account, make it somewhere you can't get at on impulse though not inaccessible in an emergency. If it is somewhere earning a bit more interest, that will be a good incentive to leave it alone. See what local banks and building societies have to offer, or talk to somebody in the know, who may have more ideas about economizing. Set yourself realistic goals. If you haven't managed that first million by the time you're 20, don't go out and blow the whole £73 you did scrape together.

Paying Bills

People who are comfortably off don't wait till six to give you a ring but you could try keeping peak calls for emergencies only, and wade through all the bumf to find out what savings can be made. Never mind the fancy extras. The 1571 'answering machine' facility is fairly cheap, but few callers like using it. Besides, 1471 is a mini answering service which enables you to check your last caller, and can save you money; if the message was that important, they'll call back. If you don't recognize the number but ring up, you'll only get two people with no idea to whom they are talking.

Arrange for an itemized phone bill; the subsequent sheaf of paper should shock you into cutting down on calls. As is the thought of one penny of your hard-earned cash going to pay any actor who repeatedly informs you 'it's good to talk'. Find out about other services, like cable. Talking does not come cheap, except for those who would rather hold a short-tempered lobster to their ear than a telephone. If you're liable to spend hours on the phone, invest in a timer, or persuade your children to remove you bodily after a set time. You can look forward to the pleasure of returning the favour.

Paying by Direct Debit

All bills can be paid directly from your bank account or your building society; smaller, regular amounts seem more bearable than colossal lump sums. You still need to make sure of putting aside enough to cover the instalments, which isn't always easy, while paying out extra 'interest' to the organization involved is galling, when the convenience is as much for their benefit as for yours. *Always* check their sums. For example, British Gas initially calculate from your last five payments, making sure they're covered, the surplus being credited to your account after twelve months. Any discrepancy, for example, a sudden surge in demand, and they immediately increase the debit, sometimes with little warning. So before you invite your penfriend to stay for a month (the one who feels the cold and has three baths a day), remember the next bill will be steep, plus you have to convince the gas company this is not typical so there's no need to double the amount due.

Debt

Money causes rows in all households, and debts often result from divorce. Over two million people have problems; there's an average of approximately four debts per household. Even low-income households are bombarded with invitations to spend, spend, spend, and how to resist temptation, when constantly assured that we can 'pay later'? But 'later' comes along sooner than you think; instead of being able to settle your debts, you could be worse off due to circumstances beyond your control, from losing your job to paying a fortune for emergency repairs.

The frightening thing about debt is how rapidly it grows out of control. From the first time you delay or miss one payment, matters accelerate until you could risk imprisonment. Juggling payments, using money set aside for one bill to pay off another that is more urgent, may lead to incurring multiple debts and borrowing money to try and sort them out. You end up pressurized because you cannot keep up with repayments, and stress often leads to health problems, which in turn affects your ability to earn a living. Creditors resort to legal pressure – solicitors' letters, summonses, court action – putting you under threat of legal sanctions, such as seizure of goods, services disconnected or losing your home.

Few people wish to contemplate such scenarios but if you are unable to face up to the problem, things mount up. The sooner you deal with the situation, the quicker it's sorted out. More urgent debts should be settled first, to avoid legal action being taken against you or services being cut off – bills (water, gas, electricity and telephone;

mortgage or rent; Council Tax), fines and court orders. Lower priority debts include repayments (catalogues, hire purchase, store and credit cards), loans and overdrafts to banks or building societies. Returning company credit cards or cutting them up removes temptation.

Settling Debts

The total owed may seem impossible to pay off, but you can get advice (and counselling, see Useful Addresses) about negotiating terms with your creditors. Write a letter about your current situation, assuring them of your intention to clear the debt. Explain how you propose to do so and what you can afford to offer as a regular payment. Avoid trying to soft-soap them by quoting an unrealistic amount rather than a sum you can afford, otherwise you'll struggle even harder to make ends meet. The stress of that is far worse than the embarrassment of offering creditors a payment which seems ridiculously minute. Most organizations are sympathetic, providing you explain your situation and make arrangements to start paying them back. It proves you're prepared to shoulder your responsibilities, and ensures they receive some payment. If you're declared bankrupt, they may not get any money back.

The Citizens Advice Bureau (CAB) will help you draw up an income and expenditure list so you can calculate what you will be able to afford to pay back. The amount will be divided, with the largest debt receiving the largest repayment. After signing an agreement with the CAB, they contact everyone on your behalf, offering small regular payments in order to settle the outstanding debt. It's also possible to pay arrears by having money deducted from Income Support.

There have been cases of women who end up in a county court being sent to prison for non-payment of fines, although magistrates have a range of alternatives. Usually, the money you need to live on is taken into account, then the amount of repayment set, as it would have been had you gone to the CAB. For example, when I applied to the small claims court to recover a sizeable debt, the defendant offered a monthly repayment which meant they must have been living on fresh air; after expenses were deducted from income, it left them with a grand total of £7.13 per month. But the whole debt was paid off, for all 'it's hard to get a loan when you're involved in a court case'.

9

Economizing: Home Repairs and Money-saving Tips

Home Repairs

Emergencies

Theoretically, emergencies are a rare occurrence, since prevention is better than cure, but most of us have faith that things will miraculously sort themselves out, up until they pass the point of no return. With so-called built-in obsolescence, it doesn't seem worth having a ghetto blaster fixed for £30 when a new one costs £60, but keeping everything as clean and tidy as possible helps reduce the effects of wear and tear – other than on relationships, if anyone is unwilling to take turns with housework. Repair bills are horrendous, and if you don't have a basic knowledge of DIY, find somebody who does. Usually, they also have the tools for the job, which saves you buying any.

Heating

Gas, electricity and plumbing are the main things to go wrong, all three if you are truly unfortunate. An expert touch is required, and as regards electricity, this does not mean somebody studying electronics who is 'willing to have a go'. Word of mouth is best to find somebody reliable, but there are also more options in *Yellow Pages*. Remember to get at least two estimates; a delay of a day or two may be more bearable than forking out twice as much for 24-hour service.

Even small problems cause a huge amount of stress, but blocked sinks and toilets that won't flush can sometimes be sorted out quite easily. Even if you hate DIY and doing repairs, it's far worse listening to the plumber whistling while he works and raving about his new Porsche or round-the-world cruise. OK, slight exaggeration, but it's bad enough paying out a huge amount to get something fixed without discovering it's something you could have done yourself. Consider all possibilities, and never ignore the obvious. For example, if the washbasin is blocked, when checking the drain outside, look up as well, at the 'hopper' at the top of the drainpipe.

This is like a container, into which the pipes from the bath and the basin empty; if one of these pipes becomes dislodged, it may get jammed into the side of the hopper, preventing water from draining away.

Money-saving Tips

Clothing

Few things are worse than having to live somewhere really cold and it does you no good when trying to work or study because all you can concentrate on is how to keep warm. If you don layers of clothing, several thin jumpers are cosier than one thick one, and can be gradually discarded as you warm up. Wrapping a scarf around your neck or a shawl round your shoulders may make you feel like an idiot, but at least you're a warm idiot. You could also wear two pairs of socks or a combination of tights and socks, plus a pair of fingerless gloves, inside and out. When going out, a hat stops heat from escaping via the top of your head. And never mind salads, which are more expensive in winter anyway; warm yourself up with potatoes, pasta and stews.

Heating

Reducing the temperature by turning down the thermostat just one degree saves about 10 per cent on your annual central heating bill, and whenever you leave the house, turn the heating off or down low, according to how long you'll be away. Siting the thermostat somewhere chilly keeps it working overtime, making warmer rooms stifling. It's not particularly healthy having the house roasting hot 24 hours a day; if the heating comes on half an hour before you get up, and is turned off an hour before bedtime, when the building is thoroughly warmed up, that should still keep you cosy. Naturally, it depends whether you're prone to feeling the cold. Some people waltz off to the pub in mid-January wearing a cardigan but no coat, yet complain bitterly if their room isn't like a midsummer heatwave.

Other ideas to preserve heat: lag the hot-water tank with a jacket, or if you can't afford one, wrap an old thick blanket or bedspread around it. Bare boards also encourage heat loss so lay carpeting which is as thick as possible. Keep all doors shut, fitting draught excluders along the bottom, as well as around your windows. Curtains which pull across doors help keep out draughts, and the gap between door and floor can be blocked off with a 'sausage-dog' draught excluder (or the leg of an old pair of tights stuffed with scraps of material).

Help with Costs

Energy-saving

The Home Energy Efficiency Scheme (HEES) provides grants to people on a low income and those aged over 60 to pay for loft insulation or draught-proofing. They also provide two free energy-saving light bulbs, which normally cost over £10 each; the outlay is recovered in about 12 months. These are best used where lights are most frequently left on, as in the hall, and in awkwardly placed light fittings, where they won't need changing as often. Waiting lists may be as long as 12 months, but if you are not eligible for a grant, local energy advice centres (LEACs) provide useful suggestions and information, including local schemes: 0800 512012. More details about the Energy Efficiency Office can be obtained from: 0191 261 5677; NEA.

Fridges

The Fridgesavers scheme provides new, energy-efficient fridges with a two-star freezer for £25 to families on low incomes, saving them about £30 on annual electricity bills. A fridge with an ice box, in a poor state of repair, means you will be eligible; those with fridge-freezers do not qualify. If you are on an income-related benefit – Job Seeker's Allowance, Income Support, Family Credit, Housing Benefit or a Disability Allowance – you can apply for a confidential questionnaire from Lothian and Edinburgh Environmental Partnership (LEEP) who administer the scheme: 72 New Haven Road, Edinburgh EH6 5QG.

Water

If a water meter has been fitted, keep costs down by putting a large bottle of drinking water in the fridge instead of wasting water by letting the tap run until it is cold. Take showers instead of baths, and use the washing machine only for full loads.

Good Buys

Whenever you need to buy something urgently and have next to nothing to spend, it's heart-warming to think that there's always a constant turnover in goods. Bargains are not that hard to track down.

What one person can't wait to be rid of frequently proves to be a godsend for somebody else. Keep an eye on the articles for sale section in the local paper; advertisements on the radio; postcards in shops and supermarkets. Numerous places have sprung up, selling seconds, bankrupt stock, goods intended for export, plus the £1 shops, some of which just put in an appearance for the summer season and at Christmas. Watch out for special offers on things like the more costly winter items – clothing, bedding and quilts, heaters, etc. – purchased out of season, they shouldn't cost as much. False economy is buying something cheap which doesn't last two minutes; thrift means thinking ahead. Initial expenditure may be costly, but it's worth it in the long run.

10
More Money-saving Tips: Food and Shopping

One diet is guaranteed to make you lose weight – poverty. But don't add to your problems when you're hard up, especially as forever fretting about your weight is liable to have an adverse effect on your children, including sons. Anorexia is an increasing problem with young men. And no point worrying about healthy eating because the jury is forever out on that one. Remember when potatoes were the villain of the piece, or rather, the menu?

Menu-planning

When money is a problem, panicking over food becomes largely irrelevant because your main aim is to buy whatever's the best value for the entire family, rather than having nightmares about BSE, additives, preservatives, or whatever is *nouvelle* flavour of the month. However, if you end up preparing separate meals for everyone to avoid wastage, that's time-consuming, and an excellent reason for anyone wanting something different to learn to cook it themselves. With many youngsters, if you are what you eat, a lot of them must be junk. Regardless of the experts, particularly when they're busy disagreeing with each other, most of us have some understanding of nutrition, so it's down to using common sense. Economize by buying fruit and veg from a greengrocer rather than choosing the nice, shiny, expensive supermarket packs. It still has to be washed, so why pay extra? In the summer, combine business and pleasure by picking your own. Pasta, rice and potatoes are relatively cheap and very good for you, as well as filling; vitamins and minerals should be included as well.

Good health is most important, not least because prescriptions, dental care and so on can be exorbitant. The harder you work or study, the hungrier you get and working up an appetite affects your concentration. After a meal, you'll get a lot more done and have more energy to do it, but a huge amount to eat means you won't feel like buying more food if you then go to the shops. Unfortunately, you spend a small fortune if you go shopping on an empty stomach; one big weekly shop saves money and time. Keep the receipts to calculate exactly how much you spend; a surprise dinner for your best friend's birthday is a nice idea, but not if it costs £25. Stick to your list of essentials and you shouldn't end up infuriated, having to traipse back out again because you forgot the one thing you went to buy in the first place. If you collect money-off coupons, some stores cough up even when you haven't bought said product. A drawer full of vouchers is a nuisance, but people don't always bother taking advantage of them, so if there's a lottery element, it improves your chances of winning.

Shopping around

It's a nuisance having to spend your time looking for bargains, calculating the cost of similar products and trying to work out what that is per gram (and how much is a gram anyway?). You may have to go out of your way because the corner shop doesn't stock a cheaper brand or certain items cost much less elsewhere. Look for the reduced goods displayed in supermarkets: dented tins, squashed packets, end of lines (always one of your favourites, for some reason). Own brands are usually low-priced because of inexpensive packaging, but while some are nearly as good as the real thing, other products taste disgusting; it's trial and error. Take bread, which is so cheap in all supermarkets, they may as well give it away. Most other customers seem to think it *is* the best thing since sliced bread, though it's usually stale by the time you get home.

Cuisine nowadays is virtually the eighth art, although not everybody is mad on cooking meals. But it is better for you, cheaper than convenience food and time-saving, if you make double portions, keeping some for another day. Weekly menus are likely to be according to supermarket offers, and if this requires bulk buying (buy 17 tins of catfood, get one free), round up your friends, particularly the one with a car. Even with next-to-no storage space, you can never have too many toilet rolls, and other own brand better buys include toiletries (soap, bath oil, shampoo) and stuff for the house (washing-up liquid, polish). You may need a helping hand with soap powder and softeners because, for some reason, the big packs cost the same as ones half the size. At least they keep the washing machine going for ages, though not necessarily as long as they're said to do.

Occasional trips to discount food stores are also handy, although you have to buy in bulk, and most places can be offputtingly grim. Concentrate on their special offers, to add a little variety to your menu. Back to supermarkets, where the last half-hour before closing is a good time for bargains. Food is reduced to next to nothing to clear the shelves – mainly bread and cakes, occasionally meat and items from the greengrocer section (likewise fruit and veg in the market). Sell-by dates have done wonders to improve the average menu, and eat-by dates give you even more leeway, so you don't have to stuff your face the minute you're home. Be cautious with foodstuffs like prawns, rather than risking food poisoning for the sake of an unexpected treat.

As for the money put aside for a rainy day, if people haven't ventured out because of the weather, stores are stuck with loads of food to get rid of, and bring prices right down. Likewise, prices drop after bank holidays, particularly Christmas and Easter, and you can stock up with out-of-season goodies. Delicatessens or food halls in department stores also have bargains, food which was presumably originally destined for export, judging by the cooking instructions (make sure there's an English version). Avoid the crowds at supermarkets at lunchtimes, Thursday and Friday nights, and especially before bank holidays, when people panic like they're auditioning for a part in a disaster movie. They can't all be having the whole family to stay for the weekend; maybe they haven't noticed stores rarely close any more? The shopping must go on.

11

Life's Little Luxuries: Clothes, Entertainment

Clothes

One person's luxury is another's necessity; for some people, clothes, and lots of them, are the stuff of life, others take no interest as long as there's something relatively clean lying around to wear the next day. And there's nothing wrong with labels, providing they don't say 'dry clean only', don't cost miles more than you can afford and aren't attached to something everyone else is wearing.

Clothes needn't be expensive. Shoes, boots and trainers aren't that cheap, but nearly everything else can be yours for next to nothing at jumble sales, closing down sales, charity shops and discount stores. Ignore undies or nightwear unless the original label is still attached, but brand new footwear or jeans do turn up in charity shops because many people prone to impulse buys fortunately have more money and, better still, taste, than sense. Small towns sometimes have up to half a dozen charity shops; look round to see which stocks the widest range and most reasonable prices. Some charge double the amount of others. Age Concern is quite reasonable, and so are animal charities like the PDSA.

People with a gift for tracking down bargains have always benefited from charity shops, but with the boom of the past few years, you are likely to find at least one item worth having, for example, a £30 dress reduced to £2.99 because it had two labels: size 12 and size 14. Coats and jackets, including leather, are usually the best buys, like a Next winter coat for a fiver (originally well over £100). Tops and sweaters come in useful, but buy a size or two bigger, especially with jumpers, to allow for shrinkage during washing. With dresses and blouses, you're spoilt for choice.

Local dry cleaners sometimes have a rail of unclaimed items, where you pay only for the cost of the cleaning. And if you give your wardrobe a good sort out, winter and summer, anything half way decent can be taken to the local market. If second-hand stalls aren't prepared to buy them, they could agree to a swap, similarly dress agencies. These are no longer as common, having had to compete with charity shops, so your best bet is evening wear, though you only get a couple of pounds (eventually) for any sales. You may not fancy scrambling around jumble sales, but offer to help out and you get the pick of the clothes when the stalls are being set up. Drop hints to your wealthier friends about donations for the less fortunate.

Entertainment

Going out comes high on the list of priorities for teenagers, usually at the top, but you should also make the most of it; as you get older, the opportunity may not arise. It's frustrating when there's an abundance of things to do and not enough time in which to do them, or to afford them. Art galleries and museums are generally free of charge, but the trip into town needn't cost a bomb. If you're thinking of looking for work, there'll be some perks with part-time jobs in the cinema, concert hall or leisure centre. Most places are always looking for volunteers; even if unpaid, you may get something towards expenses or a staff discount. Concert and theatre tickets are often cheap on quiet nights like Monday, sometimes half price on the night, and if drama is a favourite, you get to watch plays by helping out in the theatre. Again, lack of funding means little or no payment, but people are needed to act as ushers, or chase up props, even to do research for programmes.

Payment in Kind: Writing Reviews

Those who are good at English will find there are several outlets for reviews: student or listings magazines, local press or radio, even *The Big Issue*. There are likely to be more people queuing up to tackle music, software, film and video than books and theatre, and little choice, unless the editor can be persuaded of a need for a cult page, which should give enough leeway to obtain a few favourites. Work of this kind also comes in handy for your teenage children. If very fortunate, there's the possibility of restaurant reviews (just make sure the management have agreed to provide a complimentary meal or you'll end up doing the dishes). Similarly, if you enjoy eating out, keep your eye on the local papers since there are often special offers available, or else save up for the well-loved teatime menu. For that special occasion, one quick way to check whether a restaurant is expensive is to look at the price of dessert; if one portion costs as much as an entire supermarket offering, you'll end up forking out an arm and a leg for dinner.

12

Leisure: Activities, Hobbies and Interests

Taking it Easy

According to a recent survey, the average woman spends five days reading each year while men spend four and a half days doing that – and 17 days 'doing nothing'. No woman alive admits to that, let alone does it. We are very good at keeping ourselves constantly busy, and that's what the world (and his wife) expects of us, by which I mean the media, notoriously newspapers. But invest 100 per cent in husband and/or children, and without them, you're left bankrupt.

Everybody needs a chance to develop something uniquely their own. To have a special talent and be unable to do anything about it is one of life's great tragedies, or is it worse to be a person who is unable to accept that they have anything to offer? Most women have a huge list of priorities, with whatever they want at the bottom in the small print. Before long, they don't bother reading it.

Conversely, a new interest can become an obsession, with everything else fitted in around it, including your family. As with everything, balance is required. Take housework. Even women working from home cannot get cracking with earning a living until dishes are washed and housework done. Don't take to heart what Quentin Crisp said about dust getting no worse after four years, but keep it in mind, and reduce housekeeping to the minimum. Ask for a hand with the washing-up. *Don't* drop hints; no matter how broad, they're always too subtle for anyone else to grasp. You can always make your point by just doing your own dishes. How is it that in most households, the one who makes the least mess is the one who does the most tidying up? Expecting children to clear up after themselves is not wickedly unnatural, though it takes getting used to because you can do it more quickly and efficiently (who's had the practice, after all?). If this is your son's sole domestic qualification, his future wife will adore you.

Developing an Interest

Nowadays, two of the main growth industries are leisure and information, so it's straightforward enough finding out about something that appeals to you and where it's available. Draw up a rough programme of the average day (or week, if you're feeling ambitious) to slot in some time for yourself. This is easier if you're at home rather than working 9 a.m. to 5 p.m., though you then have the worry of affording it. Young children play and sleep and attend playschool or school, and teenagers are rarely spotted, what with studying, television and computer games, and that perennial favourite: 'Out'. Try not automatically to schedule spring-cleaning or turning out the kitchen cupboards while the children are happily occupied. They mightn't even notice. Younger women are more used to including themselves in their lives, but it's still a novelty to 30-somethings and upwards. And if you should then find there's no time for any housework, and 'basket' is a euphemism for the rising tirade of laundry, well, think again and arrange a more flexible programme.

Time for Yourself

Working women are often weary, and lack of energy clobbers motivation unless you build up your health before trying to fit yet another item into a crammed schedule. The occasional half-hour of simple pleasure may also result in a sense of well-being which makes you believe you could take on the world. You can't, of course, so don't get carried away. But at least whatever's the opposite of that doom-laden phrase 'self-fulfilling prophecy' comes true: taking time off for yourself gives you a boost, helping to make the most of life at work and at home. Aim for one period each week to energize, one to relax – that is, some form of exercise and something creative. This shouldn't be simplified as 'active' and 'passive', though exercise is never passive. Nor is relaxation, for those thinking they could just about manage to slump on the sofa, once there's something decent on TV. Reading a book isn't necessarily a passive activity when it makes you think or use your imagination; the mind can also do with the occasional work-out.

Exercise

You may want to skip this if you always hated games. All those hours at school, cowering at the back of the gym, hoping nobody expects you to perform some ridiculous stunt (all games teachers must take a degree in sarcasm). If convinced you loathe exercise, try to forget all the torture you underwent: netball on freezing mornings, sweating cobs playing tennis, in and out of the showers in 30 seconds so you shivered damply throughout the next lesson. Concentrate on the things you quite liked, although most things are bearable in half-hour sessions. If all else fails, most people enjoy dancing, and all you need is an empty room and some decent music.

Creative Activities

There's lots of potential here, even if your heart sinks at the thought of dabbling with watercolours or doodling poems. There must be something you used to enjoy, or fancied having a go at, and it's just for you, not for public display, unless that's what you're aiming for. These suggestions are initially therapeutic, to make you feel better by providing a release from daily problems. When you find something which suits you, it can then be developed as a hobby; many people made redundant have taken on a new lease of life, with the opportunity to turn a hobby into a career.

As for the value of writing, how often are people advised to make lists, pros and cons, to settle a dilemma? To write letters, either as a rehearsal or a replacement for words they feel unable to express? To keep a diary, to clarify things or get them out of their system? Again, anything artistic is excellent for stimulating the brain, and is not a passive activity. If the idea of a solitary occupation doesn't appeal, a more sociable activity like a drama group or evening class might suit you, even if you are convinced you could not possibly fit another thing into your life. It won't always be the case. If you get in the habit of denying yourself some personal space, then when you're older, retired from work with children leading their own lives, you'll have plenty of time on your own and no idea how to fill it. That's a worse scenario than the busiest lifestyle.

Part 3 Children

13

The After-effects of Divorce

Happy Families

While 57 per cent of people think those who want children should get married, 55 per cent believe that mothers should stay at home with children under five. It's assumed that a single-parent family never functions as well as one with two parents; the children are doomed from the moment of divorce, with no chance of leading fulfilled lives. According to one report, people who are in their twenties when their parents split are socially and economically disadvantaged, regardless of the family finances, whether well off or hard up. Children are said to be more likely to be unemployed, get divorced, make and break cohabiting relationships. Yet only slightly more than half of all young people want to get married, while one in six would live with a partner. Apparently, more boys than girls think single parents do as good a job as two parents, and most young people want to grow up to have a good family life and a job. The majority think marriage means more security for families, and nearly all of them think men and women should be equally responsible for children.

No family is ever completely free from some kind of strife, usually emanating from the same causes. It's one of the staples of the novel and, to quote a phrase used by writer Ramsey Campbell, due to 'the constant picking of motives', which inevitably winds up in a vicious circle because there's no solution. Any remark is open to interpretation because we approach things from our own way of thinking, backed by our knowledge and experience, which differ for each individual. Arguments beween children and parents revolve around chores, staying out late, money, etc. Couples who are no longer in love or particularly friendly may stay together because of their children, but the resulting atmosphere is unlikely to be more conducive to their upbringing than that in a single-parent household, where children have to cope with parental absence, economic hardship and possibly spousal conflict.

In all families, the greater the conflict, particularly between parents, the more the children suffer from health problems and low self-esteem, especially girls. Smoking is also more likely. Where stress is concerned, family life could have more effect on health than material factors or cultural influences. Children tend to do less well at school and are less likely to become college students, while there is more likelihood of problems, for example, early pregnancy. Matters improve if more time is spent with the rest of the family, for example, at meal-times or watching TV.

Divorce has more effect on older children, who are liable to blame themselves, than on pre-school children, who may not have built up much of a relationship with the father. They are more flexible and become closer to their remaining family, receiving more support from brothers and sisters, as well as their mother. Boys have more problems than girls when the mother is head of the household and becomes more authoritarian, though this is usually improved by intimacy and moments of equality. Mothers can be tougher on difficult sons, who respond with more aggressive behaviour, while girls grow more personally frustrated. Mothers with partners are more likely to be aggressive than married mothers, but adolescence spent living with mothers alone tends to result in more frustration and aggression.

Matters Maternal

Let's face it, mothers are meant to take on every role, from serene Madonna when children are babies, to a kind of benevolent oracle when they are adolescents. Nobody seems to acknowledge that women who are wonderful with babies may be out of their depth coping with teenagers. They are expected to adapt with each stage of a child's development, using their expert touch to soothe the terrible two-year-old or to encourage the reluctant schoolgoer and so on, though not all women find it easy to have a steady relationship with all their children, regardless of age. A mother is a mother, whether completely at a loss with a howling baby, or lost for words in a ferocious argument with a budding anarchist.

Every woman is deemed to keep one ear cocked for the alarm going off on her biological clock, and, being female, is assumed to be maternal. Instinctively, she knows exactly how to treat her child, no matter what the situation. Nor were women ever given much warning, though nowadays there are books and magazine articles to study about bringing up children. However, even a woman who has never regarded herself as maternal can make a pretty good attempt at bringing up her children. It may, in the long run, prove easier for her than for the woman who always wanted babies and is consequently more concerned, not just about making a good job of it, but being seen to do a good job. Few people are reticent about voicing an opinion about the correct (indeed, the only way) to bring up children.

Women in their twenties are now choosing to be sterilized, convinced that whatever life holds, they are not going to be left holding the baby. For centuries, a woman's lot was to get married and have children, and careers became a possibility only in the past hundred years or so, but many people (women as well as men) still firmly hold to the view that a woman's place is in the home. Many girls leave school thinking about getting some kind of job or attending college or university. Until they get married and have children.

Playing at Mummies and Daddies

The main aim of most parents is to do their best for their children; unfortunately, instead of being their joint concern, when parents fall out, they may use the children as a highly effective means of getting back at each other. Well, it's virtually impossible to act like civilized human beings in certain circumstances, particularly when each parent blames the other for, or accuses them of, bad behaviour. If you feel you are totally in the right yet you are always being made to feel totally wrong, saint-like behaviour vies with loss of temper, although, as we say so often to our children, you can only do your best. It takes a long, long time for most children to get over the effects of divorce, especially with parents behaving badly.

There are actually two sides to 'Public Enemy No. 1'. How your former spouse treated you is one thing, how they are with their children quite another; stick to communicating with the parent. Some parents, for various reasons, lose touch with their children, and if this is seen as rejection, it's more unbearable than the trickiest of relationships. Nearly three-quarters of children remain in contact with both parents after divorce, less than half when couples cohabit, and although there tends to be more bitterness between a formerly married couple, they provide more support for their children.

Once children grow up, how they get on with their other parent is no longer really anything to do with you. Problems more often arise with younger children, subjected to erratic behaviour: thoughtlessness (turning up late) and munificent treats (trips to Disneyworld). Parents cannot bear their children to be hurt. If such behaviour mirrors the way your Ex used to treat you, your reaction may have more to do with previous experience rather than the current situation.

While it's something of a relief not to have your Ex around, don't overlook the fact that the children will miss them, and they shouldn't have to worry about anything which may be construed as disloyalty, by either parent. It is very difficult for children to try and sort out their emotions, let alone attempt to communicate them. Dilemmas can arise which may never have occurred to you. A child feeling guilty for not trying to patch things up may end up more stressed when becoming aware that for their parents to get back together again would not be the best thing in the long run. A 'damned if you do, damned if you don't' scenario of this nature is hard enough for adults to sort out let alone a child.

When the situation continually causes upset, you may be convinced your children would be better off having less contact with your Ex, or even having nothing to do with you. Indeed, both fathers and mothers have come to the conclusion that they are doing their children more harm than good and, usually with the best of intentions, withdraw from their lives. But that's harder for children to deal with than constant rows and upsets. Even if tantrums and sulks suggest that the child does not want to be with the other parent, they *are* only children and, naturally, they behave childishly. You're the one who's meant to be mature, making sensible decisions.

Stepfamilies

Jealousy, being one of the most pointless yet painful emotions, often bedevils relationship split-ups. Any parent jealous of the attention the children give their Ex will have a whale of a time because of the latter's new partner. Some envy what they see as the other's newfound freedom, particularly when they reinvent themselves, as is often the case. Children are likely to be jealous of new partners, especially when there are also offspring on the scene. About 18 million children and adults live in stepfamilies; since jealousy stems from insecurity and divorce provides gallons of the stuff for everybody involved, it's easy to see how problems can arise.

You also need to exercise tact, preferably on a long leash, on occasions which require the presence of 'one big happy family' – parents' evening, carol service and so on – but it may be easier to take turns to attend. The last thing children need is parents who are either brawling or smarmy in front of all their friends. Even when it's difficult to be affable with your Ex, try and come to all the necessary agreements before you come to blows. Arrangements need to be regularly reviewed, especially once the children are school-age and decisions are required about education. If it's really that bad, write it down. Not having to deal with you face-to-face may also be a relief for them, though this is about compromise, not confrontation, to ensure that life goes on much the same as it used to, only with much less tension. In time, you and your Ex may communicate better. Besides, men often leave such matters to the mother, just as they do when they're married.

14
Childcare

Aims of Childcare Provision

The UK is one of the worst countries for childcare provision in Europe, especially for under-threes. Parents of under-twos in Norway, for example, have a choice of a state-run kindergarten place or a monthly payment of about £350. In this country, there are six million children under eight, but fewer than 700,000 registered childcare places. There are also about 200,000 'nannies' in all, who are not governed by the 1989 Children Act; cheaper childcare is better regulated.

Childcare tends to be seen as somewhere to dump the kids from 9 a.m. to 5 p.m. Problems with provision mean that communities are also affected, because working mothers are unable to help with schools and other groups, and three-quarters of them want something better – ideally, what's best for children from birth to eight, while providing support for parents who work. The main aim is care which is demonstrably safe and good for the children and which sets standards, for example, the difference between right and wrong. Currently, the onus to arrange suitable childcare is on the parents, but if the government set high standards to ensure consistency, this system would guarantee a network of high-quality carers who receive ample support and resources. Childcare agencies are not always well organized and many carers are not fully qualified. Employing those from other countries can lead to culture clashes, especially over religion, and home-based care runs the risk of abuse. The ideal is seen as community-based care, a sort of advanced playgroup but less institutionalized. A new pilot programme for three- and four-year-olds provides education and daycare; thus child and parent benefit.

Childcare Arrangements and Costs

Finding the right person is extremely time-consuming and nerve-racking; conversely, if your daughter decides to work in childcare, you may feel it's hardly ideal, involving young girls being sent out to 'strange' families. Worse still, because of the amount of information available about families, details have been passed on for criminal purposes. With the professional classes, 18 per cent of childcare is carried out by grandparents, 44 per cent for the unskilled, and two-thirds of single parents. In all, 45 per cent make informal arrangements. Costs can take up 20 per cent of married parents' income (nearly 100 per cent if part-time), and used to be about 50 per cent for single parents, although greater provision is now made for those claiming Family Credit. In London, women need to earn £40,000 a year to afford childcare, and nannies are sometimes better off than the mother. One year's childcare, with one child at school and one at home, costs around £6,000, 50 per cent more than the food bill.

Childcare can mean a range of services, depending on your job or changes in employment. Similarly, children develop different recreational and educational needs. Childcare requirements also vary, according to age. Continuity is important, to provide security, but problems arise with the high turnover in mothers' helps and au pairs, as well as in staff at day nurseries. Special needs have to be taken into consideration, plus considering what's best for children who flourish on a one-to-one basis and those who enjoy being in a group with other children. The former may be better looked after at home; the latter do well going to a childminder, day nursery, nursery class or crèche.

Choice of Childcare

When calculating how many hours are required for childcare, remember to include the extra time spent getting everyone ready, then delivering your child to the carer, especially in the morning. Then add the time spent commuting, and extra babysitting if you work late. It can be difficult if your working pattern varies due to shifts, holidays or job-sharing, so investigate any possibilities at work, such as flexitime. When job-sharing, one solution might be to share the childcare as well. Some employers, particularly educational establishments and health organizations, provide crèche facilities, which may be on the basis of a part-time nursery.

There are about 1,500 after-school clubs in the UK (see Useful Addresses, Work, Kids' Club Network) and the government plans to double this figure. They cater for children aged five to 15, frequently on school premises, but rarely provide educational activities. Although they are usually registered with the local authority, this is not required by law. Holiday playschemes are also organized by these clubs but the hours are not flexible and you cannot specify your child's needs.

Social services have lists of registered local childcare (day nurseries and childminders), but if you're working full time and the house is big enough, you may opt for live-in childcare, perhaps from a member of the family. Even if unable to return this favour, there are other ways to help each other out, from running errands to simply providing some company. If employing a nanny, to keep costs down, consider sharing her services with another family – whether she takes turns looking after the children or all of them together – or include another parent who just needs part-time childcare.

Mothers' helps either live in or visit daily, doing housework and sometimes cooking and shopping, but should not be left in charge of pre-school children if untrained. Nor should au pairs (unmarried girls, aged 17 to 27), unless they are qualified. They may sound exotic, but could keep an eye on older children, since they live as a member of the family. Generally, they receive an allowance of about £40 a week, plus a room and two days off, in return for five hours work a day. Au pairs are most unlikely to provide any educational activities (other than a few choice words in a foreign language), whereas this is a possibility with other carers, most usually those in nurseries.

Here, if a carer falls ill, somebody can take over, though if you're not well you will have to arrange for the child to be delivered and collected. The same situation will arise with a childminder, and any illness there means making other childcare arrangements. However, specific needs can be taken into account at a childminder's, with more flexible hours and childcare available during the holidays, when some nurseries are closed. Childminders can take care of up to six children (occasionally including their own), from babies upwards, at their home. Nurseries don't always take babies, the usual minimum age being two, and there is considerable competition to get a place in local council nurseries. Priority is sometimes given to children of families in difficult circumstances. Other nurseries are run by communities, charities and employers; the latter, though intended for staff, may take other children. Sometimes primary schools also run nurseries.

Assessing Childcare

The 1989 Children Act set down guidelines for good childcare practice. Ken Adams's book *Bring out the Genius in Your Child* (Ward Lock, 1997), for all its awesome title, gives an excellent idea of the kind of activities your child should participate in for a good start to their education:

- Good relationship between the adults and the children in their care
- Cooperation between parents and carers
- Agreed policy on behaviour and punishments, with all staff trained for emergency procedures and a first aid box readily available
- Programme planned in advance, with appropriate and varied activities for all the children; physical, cognitive and social skills should all be encouraged
- Planned activities should include suggestions from the children while allowing them to work at their own pace and be treated as individuals
- A variety of toys and equipment: books, arts and craft, dressing-up and music, construction toys, jigsaws, sport and games
- Outings and visits for school-age children.

Once you have drawn up a list of possible childcare facilities, rather than making an appointment, call in. The way the person in charge reacts to an impromptu visit gives you some idea about the childcare on offer. Make a note of the atmosphere, the way both the children and the carers behave, and what activities and facilities are available. If first impressions are favourable, you needn't stay long; arrange to call back to find out more, preferably at the start of the session. You can then watch the children settling in, and put your mind at rest about bringing your offspring. If possible, don't bring them with you prior to this so you can give the situation your full attention but arrange a couple of brief visits before they start full time. This way, you can judge whether this is the best place, and give them the opportunity to become accustomed to new surroundings. You'll soon know if you've made the right choice, once the child looks forward to going and keeps talking about what they have done. Especially when they start informing you, 'But Miss So-and-So says . . .'

15

'We Don't Need No Education'

Happy Days

As with health, education is a contentious subject; there's frequently controversy about the way children are taught. Nowadays, most start school at four, which has led to the closure of some voluntary playgroups and consequently less provision for two- and three-year-olds. Children abroad don't usually go until they're six (seven in Denmark), and an early start may not make much difference. In fact, one disadvantage is that in reception classrooms, the ratio is about one adult to 35 children (two adults, if the teacher has a helper). In private playgroups, it is one to eight, with one to thirteen in state-run nurseries. If parents want to help with teaching their children, there are ample resources although, for many people, browsing in a bookshop is a kind of hell. Research suggests that about 8 million people between 16 and 60 are functionally illiterate and innumerate; one adult in six cannot read adequately while one in three is unable to do simple arithmetic. So many school leavers lack basic skills that it costs industry billions of pounds.

Meanwhile, according to one calculation, the cost of education from nursery to university would buy a decent-sized house. And some parents are extremely competitive, wanting to bask in the glow if their child does well, particularly when outshining their friends' and family's children – even their own achievements. Adamant that their child must have every advantage which was denied them and lead the kind of life they wanted to have, they disregard the child's own ambitions. Single parents who already feel stigmatized by divorce can't bear the idea of their children being failures, further proof of their shortcomings and that they can't even bring up their kids decently. Every success for the child is seen as garnering brownie points for them.

Single parents suffering from depression may imbue their children with a sense of hopelessness. Lacking encouragement and support, why should they take an interest in schoolwork? It is important to keep the school informed about the home situation; a greater understanding of any problems helps teachers to help your children, encouraging them to try and do the best work they can in the circumstances. It also lessens the risk of embarrassment or humiliation. One child, learning basic French vocabulary for the home, when told that *la chambre* was the bedroom, where her parents slept, explained that there was just her mum's room. The teacher then enquired whether her father was dead.

School Activities

Most of us know grim little anecdotes about the happiest days of our life but schools now seem far more interesting, with a greater variety of subjects, more resources, more outings. When choosing a school, check on the extra-curricular activities on offer, and whether parents are expected to be involved in meetings, social events, etc. Useful information is more likely to come from the pupils than the teachers. Parents should also be prepared to encourage children to get into the habit of doing schoolwork to the best of their ability. There'll come battles over homework and revision, but try and remember that dreadful sinking feeling at the thought of having to spend a whole hour grappling with physics. If motivation could be bottled, somebody would make a fortune.

Taking children into work has been recommended, to give them a clearer understanding of your job; one child, whose father held a senior position in the Post Office, described him as a postman. If taking your children to see your workplace is not practicable, even for a quick visit, explain what your work involves as fully as you can, tracking down suitable pictures in magazines. Working from home does give children the opportunity to be impressed by your labours, and some of your motivation may rub off. It's also useful for them to realize that you have other roles besides that of mother. Once they appreciate they can't always have first claim on your attention, any guilt about making time for yourself should disappear.

Schooling Yourself when Children Fly the Nest

Some mothers who stay home until their children start school will be raring to get a job by then. Others, rather than seeing it as a new beginning, are completely at a loss because everything has come to an end. If they do feel their only talent is for mothering, there are still opportunities: nurseries, childcare and so on, or getting involved in school activities. Extra volunteers are always welcome, especially as often it's the same people who are prepared to help. Life should be a little easier, knowing your children are at school for six hours each day, and most parents soon learn to adjust. They have the time to look for a job and go to work, or, if at home, develop their own interests.

Secondary school seems harder because you are more aware of the passing of time with your children growing up. Schoolwork becomes the real thing, rather than having fun with education. Primary teachers in the final year have the unenviable task of preparing children for the changeover, which means more involvement for parents. Worse still – exams. If your child still isn't in the habit of tackling homework sensibly, they need to get the hang of it, or they'll have little chance of learning how to revise, which is ten times more boring.

Any exam – eleven-plus, GCSE, A level or degree – is the most vital test of that child's entire life. If you're unlucky enough to have more than one sitting exams at the same time, the atmosphere is fraught because they both expect priority treatment – peace and quiet so they can work or hogging the TV so they can relax. They do not need any more pressure, so don't point out that they'll ruin their whole life if they can't be bothered to try hard enough. Exams should never be regarded as the one and only chance for success in life. Rather than nagging your children or letting them see you're worried sick, try helping them out with revision (when asked). Make sure they sleep and eat sensibly, balancing time off with time spent studying. It's hard to say whether it's more difficult with children who work themselves into the ground or those who simply won't be bothered.

16

Leisure: Children's Activities, Hobbies and Interests

But it Costs the Earth

The words most parents, single or not, dread hearing must be, 'But *everyone's* got one.' But whatever *it* is, by this time next week, *everyone's* got something else. Each Christmas, you read about parents succumbing to toy rage, always a different toy every year. Well, if you're broke, at least you don't have to turf out former favourites on a regular basis or pass them on to Oxfam. We'd give our children the world or the moon on a stick if we believed it would make them happy, and one of the worst things about being a single parent is having to deny your children things they long for, truly, deeply, madly. Fortunately, an early training in being philosophical teaches us a higher appreciation of things, especially those which don't come easily.

Difficult decisions also have to be made about hobbies and interests. How terrible to think you may be responsible for suffocating any burgeoning talent. How could you ever forgive yourself if your child did not grow up to be the famous sports star or actor they were clearly destined to be? Again, children are so ardent about such pursuits that it's hard to tell who will persevere and who will be equally passionate about something else after a month. For many mothers, quality time is restricted to the constant taxi service they provide, ferrying their offspring to after-school activities.

More than one child? Then they all have to join the same course, whether they have a knack for it or not. Well, it's not fair to leave them out. Thinking like this means parents waste a lot of time, money and energy when they go shopping and find something which is ideal for one of their children. They are then duty bound to chase up the equivalent for the others, rather than simply explaining to them that their turn will come. Being protective is one thing, but since we know life isn't fair, why let this come as a sudden shock to our children?

Admittedly, some parents do have favourites, or are inclined to be more sympathetic towards them, but spoiling one child is as foolish as overcompensating the others. If you come across an unmissable

59

bargain for one child, providing it isn't an object of desire for any or all siblings (then you really are asking for trouble), a bar of chocolate or small sum of money is always welcome for the others.

Those Little Extras

Likewise, if finding pocket money each week is difficult, save up your small change and dish it out once it mounts up to £1 or so. Children like surprises. They may moan about the number of five pence pieces but are more likely to understand the effort you've made to scrape it together, rather than your grumbles when you hand over pocket money, nagging them about not wasting it. Children are costly little things. They always seem to be asking for money for clothing, bus fares, lunch, for schooltime or leisure. It's never cheap coughing up for school activities and outings, though once the school is aware of your circumstances, you should find your child need not miss out on anything, as you can usually come to some arrangement about reduced payments. School funds may be sufficient to allow a certain number of children to participate in most activities at half the usual cost, or even free of charge. Unfortunately, ways of making such arrangements can vary enormously, from a discreet letter or phone call to the form teacher or head teacher, to schools which insist on convening an emergency committee meeting, involving the PTA, teachers and governors.

Keeping Them Occupied

Back home, there are some hobbies and interests which are free or relatively cheap. Encourage your children to take an interest in books, though they won't appreciate the wonderful advantages of belonging to a library. This has something to do with the collecting gene; borrowing a book is not as good as actually possessing it. Even more annoying, having one copy in the house is not good enough when it's a favourite with more than one child.

Artistic pursuits may involve a considerable outlay in materials, so interest your child in more economical versions. Creative writing is cheap enough, helps them out with schoolwork and may prove therapeutic. Or there are sporting activities, which again can be horrendously expensive; walking costs nothing, but is often regarded as boring. Working out at home needn't cost and it's something the whole family can pursue, if not necessarily, or advisedly, at the same time.

Keeping Pets

Pets can pose a big problem, and not just if your children hanker for a Great Dane. Nearly every child longs for something of their own to play with, while many parents regard pets as a nuisance, largely because they'll end up having to take care of them. Children go off them and get bored and can't be bothered looking after them, but you can always try a test run: if they keep to their room for an entire day, doing nothing but sleeping and playing, they'll understand better what it's like for caged animals. And never mind dog people and cat people, can you afford to buy all the equipment and keep forking out for the upkeep for even the tiniest beasties: gerbils, budgies, goldfish? If you're struggling to provide for your children, no matter how much they beg for a pet, it isn't feasible to add to your bills. Instead, encourage them to come into contact with their friends' pets when possible, or offer to help look after their neighbours' pets, perhaps taking the dog for a walk, if they're elderly or infirm (the neighbour, that is).

17
Health Matters

Households need some kind of routine, and those of single-parent families more than most, with only one person in charge. Good health is a blessing but any kind of sickness makes you feel you've been cursed. The realization that you have a sick child on your hands is always a source of worry, liable to provoke panic as much as elicit sympathy. Some children bounce along, hale and hearty, throughout their early years, while others are unbelievably accident-prone; still others catch everything that's going. And even children (2.5 per cent of those aged eight to 16) may suffer from depression and have suicidal feelings. American studies claim that children from single-parent families are more vulnerable because the family environment is less stable. There is also more pressure to succeed at school, and when mixing with more socially competitive groups.

School Allergy

Parents can't always tell when a child is genuinely ill or making a desperate attempt at attention-seeking. It's not unusual for school-children to wake up on Monday mornings with a stomach-ache or headache. Providing this is not accompanied by more severe symptoms such as vomiting, reassure them that if they still feel ill at school they should tell the nurse and, if she thinks it's serious, you'll come and get them. Since children can really be in pain as the result of stress, check whether this happens regularly. See what lessons they're missing, and whether you suspect they are being bullied. Keep an eye out for anything like this; otherwise it causes great distress, resulting in a phobia about school.

Healthy Relationships with Schools

If you decide to keep the child at home, let the school know and provide a letter once they return, as you would for appointments with the doctor or dentist. Unexplained absences are classed as truancy, which is not something you want on their record. Should they be ill enough to have to spend at least a week away from school, have a word with the teacher to see what work they could get on with. Once feeling better, some homework helps to while away the hours of convalescence, and you, the child or the school needn't worry too much about the effort to catch up. It also helps to encourage your child to keep in touch with friends, sending notes or drawings if they don't feel up to short visits or phone calls.

Packing an obviously sick child off to school is no solution even if it is highly inconvenient to keep them at home. Schools always need a contact in the event of sudden illness or a mishap, and it can be a problem for single parents to arrange some sort of back-up. In an emergency, they should be able to call upon parents (or in-laws), family, friends or neighbours; their assistance may not prove necessary but it does need to be available. If children suffer from complaints like asthma, it is vital that the school is informed, so they know what to do in the event of an attack. Don't assume this information is automatically passed on to all relevant staff members; have a word yourself with the form teacher, playground helpers and so on.

One regular problem for women is that of menstruation – irregular, if they have an unsettled cycle. Periods are also painful in the sense of embarrassment for young girls. Again, have a word with the teacher about problems like the necessity of visiting the toilets and discreet disposal. Those who have never had painful periods and enjoy rude health assume that everybody is the same and may be called upon to use their imagination. And no matter how much you suffer, try not to curse or mourn the rapidly passing years; daughters should look on growing up as cause for celebration.

Birds, Bees and Teenage Children

Many parents find it distressing to realize that a young man or young woman is a fully-fledged grown-up (which is nothing compared to the horror children feel about the fact that not only do their mum and dad know about sex but they must have done it, and probably more than once). Parents dread explaining about the birds and bees and some thankfully relinquish the task to the professionals (teachers). If young children do ask questions, try to give them straightforward answers, but don't go on at length. If they change the subject, let it be. In the last year in primary school, your consent is required (or worse still, your presence) for attendance at sex education lessons.

Your child may go off protesting that there's really no point, because you've told them all that's necessary, then come back demanding to know why you never mentioned testosterone.

Many parents think their children are bound to regard sex on a level with appetite, to be satisfied like hunger and thirst, but a lot of teenagers are still romantic enough to equate sex with true love, part of relationships, not instead of them. Whatever your personal feelings about sex education, something still causing controversy, children need to understand it properly. We assume that everybody knows everything there is to know – sex is all around us, everybody's doing it – but there's an astonishing amount of ignorance on the subject. People don't like to own up or ask for help, mistakenly thinking they must be the only person in the whole world who doesn't understand.

Most girls believe that a doctor who gives contraceptive advice to a 15-year-old has to tell her parents, while barely 50 per cent of women know that when registered with one GP, you can register with another for contraception. And unbeknown to nearly three-quarters of all women, the erroneously named 'morning-after pill' works for up to 72 hours after unprotected intercourse. Lack of information leads to unplanned pregnancies (nearly half the total) but women over 40 are more likely than teenagers to have an abortion.

The government has launched a campaign aiming for a drastic reduction in the number of teenage pregnancies, which totalled 8,000 in 1997. Girls most at risk are those who do badly at school and those who start off well at primary yet don't manage to keep it up once at secondary school; twice as many from inner cities get pregnant. The number of men prosecuted for under-age sex dropped by half in the ten years up to 1995, and an increasing number of under-16s attend family planning clinics, some of which now take only women aged under 25, even under 20.

Going back to health in general, a few books are handy but don't read medical dictionaries at bedtime or you'll be convinced you're all suffering from strange diseases. Keep a first aid kit to hand and learn the basics. Once the children are old enough, teach them what to do in an emergency. Even young children can learn simple relaxation techniques, such as breathing properly, which eases feeling faint or sick. If one of them is very ill, try to arrange for somebody to keep an eye on the others for the time being. Caring for sick children is time-consuming and worrying, followed by a convalescence period when they get bored and drive everyone up the wall, especially if they refuse to take care and the others are getting fed up and feel left out. Watch that all this hassle does not, literally, end up making you sick.

18

Teenagers: Sex and Drugs and Rock and Roll

Terrible Teens

Most prospective parents hear ugly rumours about the terrible twos, but that's nothing compared with their offspring transmuting into the monstrosity known as the teenager. It ain't necessarily so; many of them are quite pleasant, yet the media fosters an image of adolescence which is pessimistic at best and, at times, downright horrifying. It is overshadowed only by coverage of the pre-teens and the so-called underclass. There are now half a million more men than women under 30, and boys, seeing girls outperform them academically and poised to take over the workplace, reject education because of their low prospects. Increasing numbers of young men suffer from eating disorders and depression, with a substantial rise in the suicide rate for 15- to 24-year-olds.

Those who feel it isn't the children's fault inevitably hold the parents to blame, no matter how obvious it may be that poverty, unemployment, surroundings and circumstances are the main factors to take into consideration. Admittedly, parents do sometimes feel that their children are out of control long before they reach the age of 13. The old joke goes that women give birth to sons, look after them during their formative years, then complain about the way they turn out. It doesn't always apply in single-parent families, where everybody usually needs to pitch in to help out, although where the son is the eldest, he may be expected to assume the responsibilities of head of the household. Or a girl may become a surrogate mother, having to take care of the younger children. It often causes resentment among siblings, and, as with only children, can create an unwise dependency in the mother/child relationship.

Some women are inclined to be more lenient with sons than daughters, and the latter complain, justifiably, that boys get away with anything. Girls are generally more conditioned to comply, and it is always easier to get things done by asking the person who makes the least fuss. Children should be encouraged to be independent and look after themselves; a little mutual respect and understanding goes a long way. So does some attempt at being reasonable, on both sides. You may not think highly of your

66

children's opinions, but they have a right to them, even though teenagers view the world in black and white, disinclined to heed your murmurs about shades of grey.

The Teenage World

Many parents enjoy it when their children turn into real, live people, even if they don't see much of them. However, many teenagers affect an attitude which mixes disdain with indifference, as if to disguise their intense passions (in no particular order): TV, films, food and drink, computers, dance, sport, books. The height of teenage angst is the book lover's realization that there'll never be enough time to read all the literature greats, but the greatest passion has to be music, the one thing the whole world has in common. It's hard to imagine that everyone could hate all music – even if most of us do feel vehement, either way, about one particular kind – especially when teenagers like the entire street to hear their latest CD, day in and day out, and night-time too. And what's more annoying: being unable to escape listening to said CD by the latest unmentionables, or fanaticism about the music of the past decades? They make repeated attempts to walk off with your precious record collection, claiming to know far more about your favourites. Then they decide to form their own band.

Well, it keeps them occupied and thus, by implication, out of trouble. Parents worry themselves sick about teenagers because it isn't possible (nor sensible) to protect them as easily as one usually can young children from the big, bad world outside. And they're dying to get out there. You have to let them go, even if you are convinced they are headed straight for those dens of iniquity known as clubs, pubs and gigs. Most parents know more about pubs than clubs and gigs, and what you don't know about tends to be frightening. You also have to contend with their enthusiasm, the unassailable optimism that they'll have a great time and of course nothing will go wrong. Console yourself with the thought that your worst fears are in your mind; terrible accidents are always hitting the headlines, but it doesn't mean they're inevitably going to befall your children. Teenagers who have been encouraged to be independent and resourceful – street-wise – cope with tricky situations better than those who believe that they are helpless (or worse still, useless) and must rely totally on their parents, or somebody else, coming to their rescue.

Bad Company and Bad Habits

Take drugs, for example, and maybe they will; teenagers are notorious for yearning to experiment. They'll know people who think nothing of using drugs, and be in places where they're on offer. Again, that stubborn optimism will assure them that they won't get addicted, while you should know them well enough to be convinced that they've got more sense. It's pointless panicking if you discover they have been experimenting; reading up on the subject means you'll have a few salient facts and figures at your fingertips rather than hysterical tirades at the ready.

Any misbehaviour is often down to 'peer pressure'. Congratulate yourself on having brought up children with good manners and good habits, but you'll be in for a shock if you imagine that's who's going out with their mates. Playing Jekyll and Hyde is a necessary survival tactic, used by adults themselves, depending on the company they keep. You may not approve of your children's friends, but being civilized to them is no more than you'd expect of your offspring in the company of other adults. Disapproval stems from bad habits, which parents fear are bound to rub off on their children: drugs, drinking and smoking. Teenagers who work hard and play hard often get a natural high when enjoying themselves and are scornful about artificial stimulants. Alcohol, although sometimes looked on as more damaging than drugs, is far more accessible, being lawful and largely condoned by society. There's no denying that if people enjoy a drink, they like to get drunk now and again. Nonetheless, the better your relationship with your children, the better it balances peer pressure. Parents take it for granted their offspring trust them but sometimes find it hard to return that faith, or to convince their children that they do.

19
Holidays

Gimme a Break

Holidays are taken for granted nowadays, even twice or more a year, though there are people who haven't been away in ages. According to some figures, 40 per cent of the population don't even take a holiday in any given year, usually because they can't afford it or need the money for something else. Single parents often need a break more than most families, but don't exactly have the choice, and their priority is arranging something for the children. However, with the house to yourself, a change is as good as a rest. In fact, why don't *you* treat the place like a hotel, if not for a whole week, for a couple of days at least? You'll have more spare time, and should be able to save a bit of money with not having to stock up on food, toilet rolls and so on. Not exactly ample funds to splash around but enough for a day out, going for a meal or to the theatre or the cinema. Even if you buy something special for tea, or a posh magazine, some even posher chocolates and hire a video, it's hardly over-indulgence.

Suggestions for Holidays

Meanwhile, the children may be able to spend a week's holiday with their other parent, perhaps going away with them somewhere. You might want to go away on your own for a break. Or, if you're from a large family who get on well together, you could stay with them. What about your friends? Those comfortably off who have country cottages or caravans may let you stay there and, other than during the high season, it works out fairly cheaply. And it is legal for parents to take children out of school for a holiday (two weeks during term-time).

Many single parents are relatively isolated but the NCOPF produces an informative leaflet about suitable organizations and offers helpful advice – for example, self-catering holidays work out cheaper for two families. Another useful source is the Holiday Care Service, a registered charity which has a number of free information sheets, ranging from a guide to financial help to one for families with special needs. One of their leaflets is for single-parent families while another covers ideas for lower-cost holidays. You can also find out more from tourist information centres and the national tourist boards. Some universities provide accommodation at reasonable prices during vacations, and local voluntary organizations and charities also arrange holidays.

Camping is another possibility, along with caravans and youth hostelling. See if you can borrow camping equipment rather than buying it, and have a test run beforehand, rather than learning the hard way, on a wet and windy site. Not your idea of fun maybe, but children seem to find it enjoyable. If you like the sound of farm hoildays, some are good value, particularly off-peak, and holiday centres need not work out too expensive, when entertainments and facilities are included in the price. Butlin's Holiday Worlds offer the 'Single Parent Saver' for selected dates, venues and accommodation; providing there's just one adult, and it's for at least seven nights, the first child goes for free.

To Travel Hopefully

Holiday arrangements should be made well in advance, and although you used to do all the organizing when you were married, the thought of the first holiday on your own with the children can be nightmarish. So is going away and still having to count every penny. Encourage them to save as much pocket money as they can, and try and make sure you have enough to spend for yourself.

When using public transport, packing is transformed into an art form. Leave the computer at home and, if the children are being difficult, get them to cart whatever they insist on bringing with them around the house for a while, which should put them off the idea. Excitement will preclude them from visualizing any difficulties, so you need to be very patient. Likewise, when travelling. Small children do drop off to sleep eventually, but otherwise there are likely to be constant complaints, plus the never-ending 'Are we there yet?'

Keeping children entertained on long journeys means at least two bags of goodies: one of food and drink, and the other of books, activity packs and games. A Walkman comes in useful, with audio tapes of favourite books rather than heavy metal music. If the younger children have plenty of books, six months beforehand, select a few to put away somewhere; the novelty of rediscovery saves you forking out on new ones. You can now buy a wide range of reading material at reasonable prices, but the money saved can go towards other things. When you all enjoy books, this means peaceful journeys, but make the most of it and join in their games; conversation may be a welcome change if it's been something of a luxury in harassed, everyday life. However, encourage other people who show an interest in your offspring. Old ladies and young girls appear to like temporary babysitting and the children enjoy the extra attention, so you can enjoy the peace and leave them to it. Parents who make it clear they prefer grown-up talk often wonder why their children seem incapable of listening to them.

You'll need a spare carrier bag or two for all the rubbish which accumulates, plus something to clean them up with; if it's very hot, a damp cloth helps cool them down. Always allow for the fact that children consume colossal amounts of liquid refreshment, which is unfortunate when it comes to seeking out washroom facilities. Toddlers being toilet-trained delight in urgency and inconvenience; taking them in with you is a risky business as they have a knack of either jamming the door shut or flinging it wide open.

It's also advisable to pack some form of first aid kit, kept handy, particularly if anyone's prone to travel-sickness. Even in the UK, if your destination is rumoured to be sunny, bring sunscreen with you and keep an eye on the time the children spend outside; the long golden days of childhood are no longer envied. But holidays should be enjoyable, especially when it could be a while before the next one.

20
Money, Money, Money

The Cost of Living

There's one report which would provide an effective means of contraception: the average child costs parents about £50,000 for food, clothing and leisure by age 17 (including money from generous grandparents). The average 15-year-old spends about four times as much as an eight-year-old, and children pay out about one-third on food (snacks and takeaways). Children from single-parent families receive only 10 per cent or so less than those from two-parent families.

Student Budgets

When children are used to seeing you budget, they generally find it easier to get into the habit of trying to save money. With teenagers, income comprises wages, benefits or grant, perhaps occasional financial support from you and their relatives, plus special occasions: birthday, Christmas or holidays. From this, they should deduct all outgoings, based on the list in Chapter 2. Students should draw up a budget as soon as they start their course, before that nice lump sum from those kind people at the LEA disappears completely, leaving them with nothing for the rest of term. They'll need to plan ahead to avoid running short. In the excitement of arriving at university, joining the clubs and societies and discovering the bar, funds soon run out. Gigs, etc. in the student union are cheaper than in town, but even bargains cost money. Having to check all the time whether you can afford to go out is a pain, but nothing compared to the problems of being in debt, and more students leave their courses because of financial, academic and family reasons than failing exams. Fortunately, once settled in and the novelty of trying everything out wears off, they should be spending less.

Travelling Expenses

Travel is another necessity which bites deep into the teenage budget. Many invest in a bike, but the fancier it is, the more it attracts attention and the more likely it is to be stolen. People have actually been mugged for their bikes. When travelling some distance several times a week, season tickets work out cheaper than buying one daily. Students often travel at peak times, and it's handier than queueing up at the booking office just as the train's due out. Expiry dates need checking in case it's not worth renewing them a few days before the end of term.

Bus season tickets are sometimes valid for a term's travel only, though many bus companies offer discounts, making it cheaper than the train. However, the journey probably takes longer, and is frequently tiring, especially when more walking is involved. Both bus and train may be unreliable, making life even more stressful, and bus timetables can be more limited, particularly where the last bus is concerned, which means having to use the train anyway. One advantage of living in halls of residence is that late-night buses are often laid on, though taxis are practical when several passengers share the cost.

Applications for bus season tickets require a passport-sized photograph and proof of full-time college attendance; students may be ineligible if receiving other benefits such as Income Support. Valuables may have to be insured. Lost passes sometimes need to be reported to the police as well as the bus company, and replaced after seven days (many passes are handed in within a week). There's likely to be a charge, and subsequent replacements are made at the company's discretion. Students who leave their course get the balance refunded once the pass is handed back, less a processing charge.

Insurance

Your home contents insurance policy may provide cover for students' personal possessions outside the home, although this is likely to be temporary. Paying to live in halls of residence may include the cost of insurance so they should check before taking out their own policy. It's probably a necessity with rented accommodation, where the premises will be covered by the landlord's insurance for fire and structural damage (that is, fixtures and fittings) only.

The rates for covering contents can be costly, particularly for inner-city accommodation where theft is a common hazard, though it still works out cheaper than having to replace all worldly goods. It is sometimes impossible to obtain any cover at all in areas in certain cities, so hiring TVs, videos and other appliances would actually save money, if they were to be stolen. Ensuring accommodation is as secure as possible is a sensible precaution but probably won't come cheap, and students who hate to do without state-of-the-art prized possessions are better off, literally, leaving them at home. Many companies offer special packages; Endsleigh Insurance is partly owned by the National Union of Students and can provide cover for bikes, TVs, computers, travel and so on. And if you've ever wondered about the warning about 'reading the small print', make certain your children do just that with insurance proposal forms, to get exactly the right cover.

For car owners, insurance is essential but prohibitively expensive where young drivers are concerned, especially students. As with contents insurance, it depends on the area with cities obviously being pricier than the countryside, although a car is often a necessity in rural areas. Double-check when they are studying away from home, as it may be cheaper taking out insurance there.

21

Saturday Jobs ... and Slave Labour

Hard Graft

For single parents, the worst thing about having no money is that you are depriving your children of everything they want. 'Want', however, is a different thing from 'need', and anybody who wants something badly enough will think of a way to get it. Cash-flow problems are an incentive to work; in this day and age, entrepreneurial skills are invaluable. Teenagers perennially suffer from penury but there are a number of options open to them. From the age of ten onwards, children are allowed to spend two hours a day doing 'light horticultural or agricultural work', that is, looking after animals or tidying up gardens, for a small recompense.

Pocketing Money

Some parents feel the solution is to hand over pocket money on condition children do jobs round the house. You may have reservations about this because they are then being paid (or rewarded, to put it into psychological terms) for dusting and hoovering the room they made untidy, washing the dishes they've used. One compromise is to suggest payment for saving you time and effort by doing odd jobs: clearing out a room which is to be decorated or repairing your favourite trousers. Children may learn skills you've never acquired, and can be better at doing some things. Furthermore, once they get the hang of them, they could offer their services to other people, for a small fee. Where the service is required but money is short, they could try bartering. If the old lady next door can't manage to exercise her dog but is renowned for her biscuits, she may be prepared to make a batch in return for Lucky being taken for a walk. It's then up to the children whether they want to sell the biscuits or bring them home for you all to enjoy.

In Business

You don't need to study economics to understand supply and demand. Encourage your children to look at the postcards in newsagents' windows and so on, and the classified ads in the local

75

paper. Ask around family, friends and neighbours to find out what sort of work people are prepared to pay to have done. Anyone with a full-time job plus a house and family to look after is bound to have an annoyingly long list of things they should have got round to at least six months ago. That list can then be compared with what your children are able to do, and what they are prepared to do. There may even be things you could tackle. Remember, if you find ironing quite relaxing, many people loathe it. Or they may not have time to do much gardening, and if you no longer have a garden yourself but it was something you used to enjoy, offering your services means you kill two birds with one stone.

Help the children to make plans, working out initial outlay and how much to charge. Taking dogs for walks is cheaper than washing cars because of buying cleaning materials, whereas a paper round invariably means owning a bike (and a reliable alarm clock). They may need to learn more than the basics before tackling something relatively new. Once your child has a bike, it's only practical to learn how to look after it, from keeping it clean to repairing punctures. Once they've acquired this knowledge, it can also be put to good use, providing a bicycle repair service. Similarly, they could find out about looking after pets, helping out neighbours when they go on holiday, offering to clean out cages and so on.

Word of mouth is the best recommendation to maintain a steady flow of jobs but once children have had some experience, they can advertise, to build up their 'customer base'. Incidentally, helping them out is one thing but don't let yourself be lumbered with doing jobs they don't fancy or finishing off chores they don't do properly. Children soon get fed up with things but fortunately, the novelty of having money rarely wears off.

More Profitable Ideas

Most of these suggestions are suitable for outdoorsy, outgoing children but what about the studious ones, particularly if they are shy? Computer skills are an asset, and if they're also keen on design, many people would be interested in a service providing leaflets and posters. This may also appeal to artistic children, while the creative ones could make things to sell, such as jewellery or ornaments. If they prefer writing, encourage them to enter competitions or send off letters and/or fillers to magazines and newspapers; they frequently pay at least £5 for anything published.

On a more mundane level, cookery provides opportunities, since home-made food invariably sells like, well, hot cakes. People are also needed to help prepare food as well as tidying away and washing dishes. And there is always plenty of scope with house-work. As for babysitting, there's frequently a demand but anyone taking it on should have endless patience and an inordinate fondness for young children. Make sure the babysitter can get in touch with you, or another adult, in case of emergencies. However, there can be problems, especially when the parents are inclined to be irresponsi-ble. If they're always coming home later than arranged, don't pay up on time, and are prepared to have people babysit who don't know the children very well, this is liable to be one job more trouble than it's worth.

Slave Labour

The most usual Saturday job is working in a shop, and if produce is on sale, one perk is bringing home some of the leftovers. However, teenagers who are thrilled at succeeding in getting a proper job may overlook low wages or that they're doing a tremendous amount of work, spending a great deal of time or taking on a lot of responsibility, for little return. Even believers in the Puritan work ethic recognize the difference between hard work and drudgery. When continually broke, people are likely to take anything on, but that doesn't mean putting up with exploitation. If your children seem to be heading for such a situation, help them find more satisfactory employment.

Part 4 Work

22
Job or Career: What Are Your Options?

Attitudes towards Working Mothers

Once a woman gets married, she can go out to work or stay at home. Having children makes it a more complicated decision, and whatever the outcome, there will always be criticism. This applies also to single parents, though there are complex reasons why they try to manage on benefits rather than go out to work. Some would find it hard to cope after the trauma of divorce, and most feel their children, especially while young, should not have to deal with a working parent, on top of the other parent leaving. Once the children are old enough, single parents must go to work or they'll have to be supported by the state in place of a husband. Choice boils down to job or career.

When parents have spent a lot of time training or acquiring skills, their abilities should not be wasted, nor the opportunity to make use of them, though many employers still appear to be of the opinion that mothers have no place in the workforce. Considering all the efforts of women's liberation, this seemingly entrenched view is even odder as the millennium approaches. Besides, shouldn't it be a woman's right to choose whether she wants to go to work or to stay at home? Everybody happily agrees that looking after home and children is a job in itself, but it rarely receives any form of official recognition.

Job Dissatisfaction

Many people seem unaware that children were regarded as miniature adults until comparatively recently, most put to some kind of employment as soon as they were able, even if taking care of their siblings while their mother was busy. By the 1950s and 1960s, after the years when women made up a large proportion of the workforce while the menfolk were away fighting for king and country, it was widely accepted that women should content themselves running the household.

Nowadays, women find themselves condemned by the man in the street for going to work, or by the feminist on a soapbox for being just a housewife. But the workplace often means problems, particularly for single parents, who may be stuck in a job where employers are unsympathetic and colleagues uncongenial, exacerbated by less than pleasant surroundings. Add to this somewhere which may be difficult to get to or with unreliable transport, a rigid timetable, extra time needed for training, lack of confidence, as well as lack of experience, plus the extra money to pay for suitable clothing, as well as other overheads such as fares and reliable childcare.

Work often results in stress galloping around uncontrolled, without parents fretting about arranging time off to take care of a sick child or attend a school event. Men seem to be able to adapt to keeping work and home separate, though when fathers are workaholics, the situation is virtually the same as in a single-parent family. Post-divorce, it is not unusual for such children to end up seeing more of their father, and enjoying a better relationship. Working mothers, meanwhile, are often convinced their children are getting the worst possible start in life. It may happen in some cases, but there are some who tend to be either clinging or over-aggressive through having little opportunity for contact with other children and learning to socialize.

Home and Away: Learning to Adapt

A working mother is expected to arrange the best childcare available for her offspring, ensuring that their well-being is not badly affected by her career. Where she abandons her career to take care of the children, it hits the headlines, though there's no mention of the effect on her if she hated to leave the job she loved. Interestingly, statistics show that children whose mothers work part-time get the best GCSE results, followed by children of full-time working mothers, with those whose mothers stay at home coming third. Undeniably, however, the importance of bringing up children is something on which the future of society depends.

Mothers-to-be who are career women settle happily for six

months of maternity leave, imagining that they'll be perfectly able to transform themselves into career woman plus mother. Some will then be unable to tear themselves away from the nursery while others yearn to get back to the office. Nearly all of them have sleepless nights wondering how in God's name they will cope; as soon as the day job is finished, it's back home to start another. And is there more cause for panic with an infant, who (theoretically) spends most of its time sleeping and playing, than with a teenager who is supposedly always capable of studying hard and behaving sensibly?

Once people feel secure in a job, virtually nothing will shift them. If pay is reasonable, most reasoning stops right there. Besides, there is considerable prestige in being employed. Ideally, what working parents want, in any order, is good wages, putting skills/training to good use, job satisfaction, recognition in their own right, first-class childcare and independent, contented children. Real life invariably falls short of ideals, because it is subject to change. Motherhood is one role, working mother another, career woman a third, and to be successful in any of them requires considerable juggling. At different times, different priorities reign, but try to avoid taking so much on that something (anything) has to go. It is better to be in charge, making such decisions judiciously. It's easier to handle pressure when you recognize that once it passes, the ensuing lull is a chance to slow down and recharge your batteries before the next mad rush. Christmas is stressful, yet by comparison the rest of the holiday is almost boring. If there's never any let-up of pressure in your life, stop and think about why this should be, and what to do about it.

Forward Planning

As soon as you start scanning the sits vac columns and making enquiries, make some plans. Organization is the key, flexibility the oil to help ensure everything runs smoothly. Will you have enough support from your friends and family, as well as reliable childcare? How will you manage the transition from benefits on to a wage, and will that mean a cash-flow problem? What are you going to do about suitable clothes? Transport? What about the children?

Talk to them about possible changes; their life has already altered following the divorce, something which takes most children a long time to get over. With young children, egocentricity lingers where money is concerned and they can be horribly mercenary. They may agree that money can't buy happiness, but will soon point out that it will pay for lots of things to keep them happy for a while. Wages are your trump card, and having a better standard of living should be the standard response to complaints that your job is causing them great inconvenience. That said, when they play the guilty card, don't trump it by splashing out on everything their little hearts desire. You'll end up resentful because they won't always be grateful for goodies which are on tap. While avoiding the dread phrase 'quality time', even a few minutes spent together is always better value than the latest fad. For most women, to go to work or pursue a career which they enjoy doing, and come home to their children whom they enjoy looking after, is all they need for 'job satisfaction'.

23

Self-esteem: Making the Most of Yourself

Just a Housewife?

So, job? Or career? That depends on your circumstances. There are now more women at work than men, but some married women won't consider a career until the children are at school, or grown up. Once in the workplace, women with children, married or not, encounter similar problems. Chiefly, it's the small matter of self-esteem, which means learning to eradicate any thinking about being 'just a housewife', or whatever the equivalent is for a single parent. The latter has already received one huge blow to their self-confidence: if you fail at marriage, what's the point in attempting to succeed at anything else? Other ways at looking at it range from the cynical – 'OK, so now what could go wrong?' – to the more affirming, 'Well, I've come through that, so why shouldn't I have a go?' Clichés are meant to be comforting; no matter how trite, they are basically true. Obviously, if you had a particularly tough time of it, or you're still getting your life into some sort of order, a job may cause a 'make or break' situation. It's not something to rush into, unless lack of money makes it so.

Working ahead

Supposing job-hunting or seeking a career is part of your future plans, the very idea may make you uneasy, or even terrify you. What have you got to offer, after all? Sit yourself down and draw up a CV. Include educational qualifications, previous work experience and suitable abilities, such as patience, reliability, a good sense of humour. A second list covers areas you need to work on (computer skills, for example). However, these exercises shouldn't be undertaken on the spur of the moment. Unless you approach sorting out your strengths and weaknesses in a calm frame of mind, you'll have a false perspective. When we're feeling down, it's hard to accept that we possess any accomplishments, whereas in a good mood, we're sure we could achieve anything.

Self-esteem is undoubtedly buoyant when we're in a good mood, making it virtually impossible to think about being unhappy, just as it is hard to picture happiness when we are miserable. If people constantly make us sad, it erodes self-esteem, especially when we're inclined to take the blame. Left to ourselves, we may feel contented with who we are and what we do, but outside pressures easily persuade us otherwise. This is the hell of other people, those who criticize us, making comparisons which always leave us wanting. Many women spend much of their lives adopting the persona of daughter, wife, mother, lover, best friend, good neighbour. Now you are proposing to include work colleague and employee. If you are already burdened with low self-esteem, you feel you're exposing yourself to even more people. Yet, in all these roles, there is a part of the real you which has to be allowed to blossom, taking its proper place (priority, occasionally) among those other selves.

One well-known wry comment can be applied to low self-esteem: just because you're paranoid, doesn't mean they aren't after you. If you lack self-confidence, the overriding feeling is that they *are* after you, on your back the whole time. All of them. Even your thoughts are not your own because whatever you think up, there's a little voice waiting to contradict you, from family, friends and neighbours to figures of authority, such as teachers, doctors, employers. And we pay attention to what these people say, meekly falling in line with what they think is best, rather than what we'd like to do.

In *Shirley Valentine*, the heroine wonders why husbands always manage to be pleasant to people other than their wives, even when simply buying a newspaper. Just as baffling is the fact that we always hurt the one we love. Some people seem to behave with greater unkindness towards those they are supposed to love, as if 'love' gives them that right. It's so often done in the guise of being 'for your own good', advice intended to prevent you from making mistakes, something liable to cause embarrassment all round.

Boosting Self-esteem

Single parents are one of the most vulnerable groups in society, lacking the support of a married partner to stand up for them against criticism from children, parents, friends, neighbours. Yet frequently, it was the spouse who was largely responsible for eroding self-confidence. Escaping from constantly being downtrodden is one reason for instigating divorce proceedings, but taking such a step engenders disapproval, even when said spouse is the last person on earth anybody with a reasonable IQ would want to stay with. To contemplate divorce upsets the status quo, and it's greatly resented if it forces people to face up to the reality of their own lives. Some people seem truly to believe the biblical comment, 'better to marry than burn', that is, it's a sin *not* to stay married, no matter what.

But what if your burning desire is to make something of yourself? The process of reinventing yourself is not impossible, even after a lifetime of low self-image. Once you're aware that poor self-esteem is a problem – one that no amount of counting your blessings or listing your good points seems to solve – it's something to which you should turn your attention once you start wondering about the feasibility of working. There are plenty of venues for self-assertiveness courses (many of which run from January, bolstering up all those splendid resolutions), and even more choice when it comes to self-help books. These are now so commonplace that you can stick them in a supermarket trolley.

You may find yourself spoilt for choice because common or garden psychology proliferates, but approached with caution, a little knowledge is not necessarily a dangerous thing. It can be enlightening. In enabling ourselves to understand what we do and why we do it, gradually it becomes easier to make changes. Change, as every single parent knows, is one of the most frightening experiences in life, but without it we stagnate. Life was not meant for wasting, after all, and few thoughts are as painful as those we may have when contemplating the words 'If only . . .' With psychology being applicable to many areas, there will probably be somebody you know who has studied it to the extent of being able to offer advice. It's advice well worth having.

24

Making the Most of Your Skills

Having it all?

With few exceptions to the rule, the exuberant forecast that they could 'have it all' has brought a lot of career women down to earth with a huge jolt. There's little pleasure to be gained from status and wealth when you're permanently tired, with no time to enjoy yourself; it's impossible to 'have it all' without a huge amount of money and an equally enormous amount of support. Forget New Man. According to recent reports, he still isn't prepared to pull his weight around the house; that's down to home helps, au pairs and nannies. In fairness, many men now devote more time to their children, beyond changing nappies or cleaning up after them. Constantly juggling priorities is a nightmare for many women, and if they can manage two out of three, marriage seems to turn out not to be wholly indispensable, rather than children and career.

As single parents are expected to balance children and career or job, at this point, when discussing future plans, it is assumed that suitable childcare facilities have been arranged or that the children are old enough to be reasonably independent. You should therefore have some idea of the number of years available to which your working life may be devoted, which also helps you decide what you most want to do. Don't panic if you find it impossible to make up your mind at first; even by the beginning of this century, it was forecast that the days of working from 9 a.m. to 5 p.m. were numbered. More than ever, flexibility is a key requirement in the workforce; according to one set of figures, it is not impossible to have four career changes throughout your working life. Besides, as the man said, if you do not know which course to follow, then you have the choice of any direction.

What Skills?

Anybody who has been away from the workforce for some time may find the emphasis on 'skills' unnerving. Many women who have spent years doing nothing but bringing up children and looking after the house are convinced they possess no skills whatsoever. Despite the ubiquitous use of the word, many people assume 'skill' means the same as 'talent' or 'gift' – in other words, if you don't have an innate knack for something, it will prove impossible to acquire. According to the dictionary, 'skill' is in fact 'ability resulting from practice', and all the skills required for any job or career can usually be learned. For that matter, even somebody accustomed to describing herself as 'just a housewife' not only possesses many skills but, with all that practice, is also highly trained.

Think about it: organization, communication, finance and education are the four main areas in which many 'ordinary housewives' excel. In addition, over the years, they will also have picked up a lot of knowledge and had experience in dealing with a diversity of tasks: cuisine, interior design, purchasing, healthcare. In other words – cooking, cleaning, shopping and looking after sick kids. A rose by any other name does smell as sweet, but there's no doubt people are highly impressed if you use its Latin label. Making the most of your abilities is, in itself, a useful skill. And it's not cheating. In a world which thrives on hype, what you may regard as exaggeration is generally taken as the norm. No matter what skills you possess, if others remain unaware of them, that's no help to you whatsoever. Again, most parents, particularly mothers, are so used to what they do being taken for granted that it comes as a surprise to find that others, such as employers, will appreciate their abilities.

Counting on Your Assets

What are your abilities? What strengths do you possess which will be an asset in the workplace? What areas are you unsure of: things about which you know next to nothing, or have forgotten what you once knew, or which have changed considerably since you learned about them? A pen and some paper are all you need to begin the process of assessment; several books which you may find helpful are listed in Further Reading.

As mentioned previously, to bring up children is one of the most important jobs there is, even if parenting is largely the result of trial and error. And what kind of things have you learned from all this practice? By dividing your skills into three main groups (practical, creative, people), you will find that bringing up children is invaluable in many different areas and even a thorough knowledge of looking after the house can pay dividends.

25

Assessing Your Skills

Practical

Working with your hands round the house and in the garden can be very physical, requiring stamina and energy, and helps keep you in good shape. Don't underestimate the little things you accomplish; you may be trying to save time by throwing whatever's lying around the bedroom floor into the toy-box, or bits and bobs from the garden into the bin; technically, it's 'good hand-eye coordination'. You'll also have had to carry out some repairs and maintenance, maybe assemble things (bookcases) or work with tools (change plugs). Each thing on its own doesn't seem much, but put together, makes an impressive amount.

Creative

Practical and creative activities include cookery, crafts, sewing, painting and decorating. Usually these are described as talents rather than skills. How they are described depends on their purpose, and they have the bonus of being therapeutic. If you've never bought a tin of paint before, standing in a newly decorated room is extremely satisfying (providing you're far enough from any painted surfaces to notice the drips). Admittedly, some of us never get the hang of handicrafts. Any painful memories of fumbling attempts with yoghurt pots and cereal packets, turning out the worst efforts in your child's playschool, could mean your abilities do not lie in this direction.

Discovering a hidden talent with the potential to be turned into a business concern is a marvellous asset. One Australian millionairess claims the secret is simple; find something you are good at and love doing, then put everything into it. However, although most people are not good at things which they hate doing, it is possible to become skilled at something you don't actually enjoy. Even if it will make money, though, it's not the best option. An excellent cook may love food, but if the thought of working in a kitchen is depressing, is it worth doing?

Attempts to make a career out of being creative are apt to be viewed with scepticism. It can't be a proper job, although increasing numbers of people are involved in the arts, and even if pay is low, job satisfaction presumably is high. Women are often convinced they're being self-indulgent, no matter how good they are at anything artistic: designing, acting, writing, composing music. In fact, you will be setting your children a good example, if you want them to be happy, doing what they want to do. If needs be, give yourself a year, and if it doesn't work out, then think about another job. We always tell children to do their best and encourage them to reach for the stars, but don't always take our own advice.

Parents also underestimate their mental capacity, particularly when conversation over the past few years has revolved round what their eldest did at teatime and the way the price of light bulbs has shot up. Yet how often are they required to provide ideas to keep their children from being bored, or from falling out with each other? This involves thinking up different projects, which then require developing or improvement. They also get involved with their children's ideas, explaining why some aren't possible, coming up with alternatives, and enabling them to go ahead with the most feasible, adapting those which are less so.

Organization

All kinds of organizational skills, from day-to-day housekeeping to day trips, are expected from parents. Problems are always cropping up and need to be separated into the trivial and the important, that is, assessed as urgent (short-term) and essential (long-term). The actual process involves assembling all the information available and analysing it; even intuition should not be underestimated, since it means being able to predict possible outcomes.

Information

Nowadays, we are all able to acquire more and more knowledge about all kinds of things and, even if we forget, it's impossible for these details to disappear completely. Information cannot be disposed of. What complicates matters is the necessity to concentrate on the relevant. Useful information skills for parents are managing money, following instructions and having a good memory. The last may mean that the whole household regards you as the fount of all knowledge and doesn't bother with common sense. Parents are always expected to know the whereabouts of every single movable object in the house *and* its current condition. Teenagers rarely understand the concept of looking for things; told a particular item is in the airing cupboard, any attempt to locate it consists solely of opening the door and peering inside.

If you've always been fascinated by information – you are curious about all manner of things and have an eye for detail – then automatically prioritizing and classifying everything is probably a habit. The thought of computers may be nerve-racking but you'll be aware of all the opportunities in technology, and that it includes a wide range of jobs.

Communication

The last, probably most important, area involves dealing with other people, as individuals and in groups. You will have realized the benefits of dealing with your children on a one-to-one basis (not least when they decide to gang up on you). When they come to you with problems, it's easier to help them, particularly when motivating them to decide what they are going to do and how they are going to do it. With schoolwork, there's a fine line between making suggestions and virtually taking it over so that they get good marks. The better you can communicate what you think needs to be done, the more they learn the importance of how to communicate in writing.

On certain occasions, you need to mediate for your children; in problems at school, or outside school, with their friends' parents, if they fall out. Your own friends may tend to ask your advice, whether they've had a row with someone or happen to be hard up. Once people regard you as a mine of information, restrict yourself to telling them where they can find the answer, rather than seeking it out yourself, unless it's something which is of use to you.

A talent for persuasion has considerable uses; for example, as the basis of selling anything to anyone. The ability to communicate in writing now seems less important than aural communication, either face-to-face or on the phone. A good telephone manner is essential, at home and at work, yet some people still hate using the phone. Keep it short and simple, but try not to sound brusque; thinking about the money it saves should make you feel happier.

Communication with Groups

Finally, there's a lot of skill involved in dealing with people en masse, and once you start moving up the career ladder, part of your work may be supervisory. Most jobs also involve some delegation, which requires communication and organizational skills. There are pros and cons for working on your own, and in a team, where you may be called upon to suggest, comment, advise, criticize, persuade, instruct. The more adept you are, the more you'll succeed. You will be seen as having leadership qualities, which may then be tested out: leading discussions, making presentations or demonstrations, organizing activities. Managing a group means a great deal of responsibility, and it's up to you to ensure everything is done properly and on time. In addition to passing on orders from above, you may be in a position to implement your own projects, in charge of a team. That means establishing workable rules, and a considerable amount of negotiation. Does it sound exhausting just to think about? It's no more than you've already been doing all this time with your children.

26

Form-filling II: Income Tax,
National Insurance, Student Grants

Income Tax Returns

Income Tax returns are accompanied by a guide for filling them in,
but they may not be as difficult as anticipated. Very little of it
applies to you, if annual income does not reach the personal
allowance:

- Details of the business
- Income
- Interest from building society
- Interest paid on mortgage
- Pension contributions
- Confirmation that a child is living with you and you are divorced.

If need be, seek help with completing forms. Even when you're on a
low income, if you expect your earnings to increase, make a habit of
keeping receipts, filing them in order. Once expenses are taken into
account, you are expected, for example, as a freelance writer to
provide proof of:

- Train tickets (travel expenses)
- Itemized telephone bill
- Postage and stationery items: paper, envelopes, headed notepaper,
  printer cartridges.
- Subscriptions to professional bodies and publications.

The new system of self-assessment was intended to simplify matters
and you can do your own calculations, unless you prefer to leave it
to the tax office. If you are self-employed, keep the following
records:

- All sources of income
- Payments for which you will claim tax relief (payments to
  charities, private pensions, etc.)
- Bank and building society interest and dividend vouchers
- Business earnings and expenses, sales invoices and receipts.

Employees should record income and benefits such as payslips and other documents, noting any tips and expenses. Everyone is legally obliged to keep records in order to fill in a tax return, so set up a system for keeping the records; maintain it throughout the year; and retain the records for as long as necessary.

The self-employed have to keep their records for about six years, so it is a good idea to keep everything together in a tax file or large envelope.

National Insurance (NI)

Everyone receives a NI card with their number on at the age of 16. The contributions go into a fund which pays out unemployment benefits, retirement pensions and so on, thus qualifying you for state benefits, and there are four classes, levied on different kinds of income. With part-time work, overheads like fares can mean you're as near as damnit as badly off as if you did not earn anything. The more you earn, the more goes in taxes so, in certain circumstances, working doesn't even look like a viable proposition. However, although you will not have to pay NI unless you earn over a certain amount a week, gaps in your record may affect future benefits, like the state pension. It is possible to make up the difference by paying Class 3 contributions; you can find out more from your local social security office.

Income Tax, similarly, has to be paid once you are earning a certain amount, although everybody has a personal allowance, depending on their circumstances (around £3,500 for a single person). This is tax-free, as are grants and most scholarships; students and their employers complete Inland Revenue form P38 (S). If tax is due, this is done either through the PAYE Scheme (Paye As You Earn) or by assessment in April, at the end of the tax year. If you have overpaid through PAYE, you get a refund by cheque from the tax office. Students on work placement should contact the tax office to check they are exempt from paying tax, providing:

- Their level of earnings does not exceed £7,000
- They are enrolled for at least one academic year
- Attendance is for at least 20 weeks full time.

Student Grants

Whether completing an application on your own behalf or for your child, this is another form which virtually demands a biography.

Don't be put off, as it should be sent in as soon as possible; there are inevitable delays due to the volume of submissions. Never bank on grant cheques waiting there to be collected the moment the student sets foot in the students' office, since they are usually late and often go missing altogether. Some LEAs make awards for students from 16 onwards when parents are receiving benefits, and there are educational establishments which cover travel costs (you should also have been able to obtain uniform grants while your children are at secondary school).

With student grants, forward the following documents, where appropriate, when first applying. Subsequently, everything is photo-copied and kept on file; if applying for more than one child, you need complete only one form, which will be cross-referred:

- Birth certificate (one for each child)
- Marriage certificate *or* Form MS1 if parents are divorced or separated *or* confirmation of date of separation with solicitor's letter advising maintenance payments and confirmation of partner's income up to date of separation
- Form FB1 for new applications
- Form FB9 for renewals
- Form FB2 (gross income and allowances, that is, employment, self-employment, state benefits) plus P60 for company directors. If self-employed, complete Section C and submit confirmation of income from Her Majesty's Inspector of Taxes (HMIT); a provisional award may be made for the summer term pending receipt of this.
- Form FB5 Certificate of earnings (for those other than the self-employed or company directors)
- Form FB16 Certificate of benefits received (Section B has to be completed by Benefit Agency)
- Form FB15 Mortgage interest (tax relief under Miras scheme)
- Form FB17 Certificate for tax relief in respect of private pension
- Form FB5C Certificate of income from pension
- FB4 Certificate of life insurance premiums paid (other than policies taken out after March 1984)
- Form FB7 if applicant has a definite place
- Official details of term dates if course is more than 30 weeks.

Enclose a stamped addressed postcard for acknowledgement of receipt of forms. All questions which are not applicable must have the word 'None' entered in the box; all questions in Form FB1 must be answered. And they mean what they say; leave anything out and the form comes straight back.

Section A is completed by the prospective student (good practice for future form-filling), covering their personal details and those of the course. You then sign the declaration, having completed Section C, which covers every aspect of your income: pensions; interest on accounts; mortgage interest and so on. You also have to advise details of other dependent children. Disabled students may be eligible for allowances, and also receive a list of useful addresses. Compared with all this, applying on your own behalf as a mature student will seem a lot more straightforward.

27

On Course: Further Education

What Course?

Many places have community education centres, geared to help all kinds of people in all kinds of circumstances, with courses ranging from key skills such as English with computers to practical matters such as 'know your rights'. Some are expensive (over £100 to learn about local history) but many are free, like 'healthy eating on a budget'. It may be possible to obtain some funding, where the course is regarded as training leading to some kind of employment. There are sometimes concessions for those on a low income.

Somebody once commented on the fact that divorced women always go in for further education, but it appears that married women who go on courses sometimes end up getting divorced. Learning can be a liberating experience when qualifications widen your horizons and increase your options. If convinced divorce is the end of civilization as we know it, education is one of the best ways of proving to yourself that, in fact, it's a second chance to live your life the way you want to.

If you loathed being at school, however, what incentive is there to return to that environment? The educational system is constantly changing, so you aren't likely to be studying in exactly the same place with exactly the same teachers, still using exactly the same methods. If you suspect, deep down, that you never received the schooling you deserved, nor had the chance to find out more about the subjects which you enjoyed, now is the time to do it. You're likely to be surprised by the variety of courses on offer. Again, arts or leisure are prone to be regarded as indulgence, and friends and family may advise sticking to something useful, such as word processing or book-keeping. Fortunately, you should be able to combine pleasure with business and, even if it feels like going back to school, especially if you've been at home for a number of years, this is the start of a gradual process. It makes a return to work seem less overwhelming.

Apart from the cost, the length of time involved may be off-putting: two years to sit A levels, three years to take a degree. It's a considerable commitment but if you can organize your life in order to attend a course, the same routine will serve a purpose once you have a job. Many educational establishments also run short courses, some of which can be regarded as a practice run to build up your self-confidence and your social life. How embarrassing, though, sitting alongside youngsters fresh out of school, all of them up to date with study skills! In fact, classes comprise a broad cross-section of the population and, even on a degree course, technically they are mostly mature students, that is, over the age of 21 (some of them well over).

The longer courses are advertised locally in time for the September term but look for details of night school classes, which run for a few weeks. Make a list of all the local educational establishments (try *Yellow Pages* or ask at the library) and contact them for details. In view of funding problems, colleges, etc. have to compete against each other, and as a high intake of students justifies the existence of a course, few people are unfortunate enough to be unable to get a place anywhere.

Finding out about Funding

One priority is to ascertain available funding; at the beginning of the 1990s, it came as a pleasant surprise to discover that there was quite an ample grant for a mature student with three dependent children. There are always cutbacks, however, and if your children all plan on going to university, it's not unusual to discover that each year seems to bring cuts of about 10 per cent in grants. The number of eligible students may also be reduced or the issue of travel passes restricted.

Other Costs

There is more expense and time involved if you should be advised to sit GCSEs or A levels or take a foundation course before studying for a degree. You may be hampered by other restrictions: lack of childcare facilities (although many educational establishments have crèches), travelling distances, limited study options. Then there could be additional equipment to pay for, such as books and a computer, possibly field trips and outings. This could increase your overheads to what seems to be an impossible amount, so look into this area thoroughly before taking any action. Ask around for more information and speak to other people who have gone back into education to see how they managed. In general, you will find plenty of encouragement and help on offer. For example, there should be ample computer facilities on site (though it's more convenient to work at home), and although textbooks are expensive, sometimes copies turn up at second-hand bookshops, charity shops, car boot or jumble sales. Students from the year above are often willing to sell books they've finished with. It's even possible to get through an entire course without purchasing any (especially if studying librarianship), when you have recourse to well-stocked libraries on campus, in the city and locally.

Studies on Being a Student

It is also useful to read up about study skills, and about student life. Even if commuting from home, you may become involved in certain aspects of student life, joining some of the clubs and societies. There are also occasional job opportunities on campus, plus ample access to information, making it easier to find out about work. Furthermore, besides studying for your degree, you'll learn additional skills, from using computers to writing reports and communicating, even running workshops or lecturing.

And even if the other students are a lot younger than you (and some of the tutors, for that matter), it doesn't make them an alien species. There's no reason why you shouldn't get on with some of them, especially if you have teenagers of your own, which ensures that things like music and fashion are not a complete mystery. Besides, most conversation will focus on what you're actually studying, and a mixture of views is often enlightening. You will be taught in a variety of ways: lectures or seminars to the entire year or your whole class; tutorials in small groups of about a dozen; occasional assessments on a one-to-one basis with a tutor; discussions with your personal tutor.

Having made up your mind to go back into education, you will almost certainly find it rewarding. Whether just fancying a change or determined to do something different with your life, you should find yourself on course before too long.

28

'We Have the Technology, Now What Do We Do with It?' Using Computers when Working from Home

Computer Skills

Girls with no immediate career prospects always used to learn secretarial skills, that is, typing. Nowadays, it's word processing, and since information technology (IT) is virtually a core subject, learning some computer skills will serve you well in many different jobs. However, if you opt for working from home, it can be tricky to put in a full day's work on the computer, especially when the children want to use it to play games or to do schoolwork.

Even a degree in IT is no guarantee you'll know everything there is to know. One kind of computer error is to realize it was a *big* mistake buying one in the first place because PCs are a classic example of the saying: 'If a thing can go wrong, it will'. They do little for family harmony, even when used purely for games or basic word processing and graphic design. These may be your criteria when buying one, but your children will have other, bigger, better and infinitely more expensive ideas. The wider the choice, the more decisions to be made, the bigger the opportunity for falling out.

When working from home, make the most of the time your children are in school because come half past three, peace and quiet are gone for good. As noted previously, it's exceptionally hard for women to accept that once you are self-employed, working for a living must take priority over housework. Conversely, once you do accept it, fitting any housework in then becomes equally tricky. Establishing a flexible routine saves you from being nagged about everything, from freshly washed games kit to fresh vegetables gathered from the garden in time for dinner.

As well as organizing your time, you need to organize stationery supplies. In other words, hide them. Stamps and envelopes will be 'borrowed', pens disappear immediately, your best typing paper gets used up for rough copies, and there will be ink all over the place whenever the printer needs a refill. And all this is nothing compared to the way World War III erupts every time you have a vitally important business phone call.

Children and Computers

For each child who takes to computers, there's another who'd prefer visiting the dentist. Trying to keep up with the technophile means having to find out all sorts of things to explain what makes it work; meanwhile, you're encouraging the technophobe, to give them enough knowledge to get by, and instil them with confidence. Start by convincing them that switching the computer on is not the equivalent of pressing the red button which ends the world with a big bang.

It's also hard work making sure everybody gets fair shares in using the computer and that nobody spends too long at any one time glued to it, whether doing schoolwork or playing computer games. Computers are stress-inducing beasts, certainly not good for you if used for hours on end. One hazard is repetitive strain injury. Make sure that the PC is situated where you can see the screen clearly, to avoid straining your eyes, at a height which is comfortable for your back. Use an adjustable chair, if necessary.

Helping You to Live in Peace with Your PC

Aromatherapy may be conducive to a good working/family atmosphere and may be either soothing or revitalizing, according to need. Obviously, candles must always be placed well out of the reach of children. It's probably more practical to use aromatherapy oils in a warm, relaxing bath. If you are interested in this kind of thing, it may be useful to read up on *feng shui*, to check if everything in your office is arranged as harmoniously as possible. Crystals are considered beneficial, too, though perhaps not if you're short-tempered and liable to use them as ammunition. A more practical idea is to learn basic massage techniques, simple enough for the children to carry out as well. Everybody loves having their back or their neck rubbed and it makes you feel much better.

The optimum time to spend at a computer is one to one and a half hours, but that's easier said than done, since work and games can be completely engrossing. You could set a timer, since arranging for someone to remind you is likely to involve a lengthy harangue, which won't do either of you any good. Nonetheless, one day, you'll look back on all this and smile; by then, learning to be organized and acquiring motivation will have paid off, and your children will be sailing confidently through secondary school and university.

Working from home has many benefits once some kind of routine has been established, even if it does involve drawing up a strict rota for the computer, with dire penalties for anybody breaking the rules. Besides, since opting out of joining the nine to five rat race on occasion means you end up working from 7.30 a.m. to 11.00 p.m., one way to ensure everybody is kept happy is to bear in mind that you are entitled to the odd day off. Then you can leave your children to fight it out among themselves.

29

Time-management

Traditional Timekeeping

Every minute of every day taken up, seemingly for weeks in advance? Caring for the children, looking after the house, holding down a job . . . Well, there are ways to make life easier. As children, even teenagers, visiting our friends' houses, we don't really notice if things are different to what we're used to at home. Women become more aware of such things once they're involved with somebody, as do married men if anything isn't the way mother used to do it, especially in the kitchen. In your house, afters might have been left out in the kitchen after the evening meal for anyone to help themselves, then thrown away the following day, whereas in your husband's home, a cake would be cut into enough slices to last the week and put away in a tin.

Women are brought up in a tradition of housekeeping, carrying out chores the way their mother did, and her mother before her. For all the many changes, and the variety of mod cons nowadays, keeping the house in order can still take up an inordinate amount of time. And it will, if you're the only one doing it. OK, as the song says, nobody does it better, but where else would you spend so much time sorting out other people's responsibilities? Many women find it terribly hard to let go of this role and firmly believe that if they do, the world will come to a sudden, messy end. But housework, surely, should lag way behind children and career?

Time to Involve the Children

Just what's involved? Write a list, in capital letters, and hang it up somewhere your children will spot it, such as on the fridge door. What they usually see are the results of all your hard work, rather than seeing you hard at it, and their first reaction is liable to be amazement, followed by sheer horror at the thought of helping out. But if they each started by taking used wrappers and crockery back into the kitchen, that in itself would make a tremendous difference. Next, encourage them not to leave things lying around, whether dirty clothing or schoolwork.

Washing

Clothes which don't go in the laundry basket don't go in the washing machine, though your children may have few scruples about wearing jeans which should have been washed weeks ago. Children who are particular about their clothes can be shown how to use the washing machine, and to put the clean clothes on the airer; they usually grasp the concept of washing eliminating dirt but may have trouble understanding that hanging up wet washing neatly helps it to dry and prevents creases.

Cleaning

Once old enough to look after their own room, if children wish to dwell in what could pass as the set of a horror film, leave them to it. With two children sharing, somehow, one is neat, the other untidy, though the latter rarely influences the former (fortunately); a tidy person may eventually demonstrate the benefits of neatness. Most people get the hang of useful habits and it may only take a more fastidious friend (girlfriend, probably) to pass a comment, or something vitally important to go missing yet again, for the most deplorably messy person to make some effort. For a while, at least. And if you expect your children to respect your privacy, then respect theirs; their rooms are their domain. Think of the time you'll save, with no need to nag them about carrying out a massive clearing-up operation before the least bit of dusting and hoovering.

Taking Turns

Housework causes nearly as much disruption as money problems. Most children fail to appreciate that keeping the place clean and tidy makes it more pleasant to inhabit, easier to work in and helps prevent wear and tear. It doesn't occur to them to wipe up anything spilt; that otherwise milk smells, while food with red or yellow colouring in it, such as pizza, leaves a stain. If drawing up a rota in the hope that everybody will do their fair share, what often happens is arguments, with everyone convinced they're the only one pulling their weight. Instead of rows about whose turn it is to do the washing-up, draw up a list of jobs, allocating them to those most prepared to do them: hoovering, shopping, cooking; cleaning the bathroom. Include seasonal jobs, like mowing the lawn, or those which need doing on a regular basis, such as defrosting the freezer, allowing for the fact that some take longer than others or they're more frequent or not so straightforward.

Sensible discussion to convince everyone that they're not badly done by calls upon your negotiating skills, which is not a synonym for nagging. It's said women weren't born with the ability to nag; they pick it up living with husband and children, and the latter are the experts. When they want something, mothers inevitably give in, worn down by repeated requests. Conversely, children somehow hold out until, yes, mother gives in again, and goes and empties the bin herself. If children know that's the usual result, why should they put themselves out? Even if it is quicker and simpler for you to deal with anything, it makes them wholly dependent on you, depriving them of a sense of responsibility. It's not the best basis for life in the big, wide world.

Time to Test a Few Things out

You could experiment by sharing a particular task with one child. This will provide an opportunity to keep an unobtrusive eye on things (and, if absolutely necessary, even more unobtrusively put them right). Of course, *yours* is the right way, but everybody has the right to do things the way they want, as long as the end results are more or less the same. We all need to delegate, but doing everything ourselves convinces us we are superhuman. It also convinces everyone else there's no need to lift a finger, because you're always there to do everything. But your efforts will usually go unrewarded; far from being appreciated, or even impressing people, you end up taken for granted.

Doing the Washing-up

Start small, perhaps arranging help with the dishes. You may be pleasantly surprised when a tentative suggestion about doing them on Sundays is met by an offer of four times a week, providing somebody else does the cooking. Allow for breakages (after the first accident, these should be paid for) and water swamping the place. Boys never believe a word of washing-up liquid ads and get through tons of the stuff, hardly visible for mounds of foam. Nor will they think to wipe over the top of the cooker or any work surfaces until you mention it, and it won't be the mini-spring-clean you're accustomed to carrying out. But you will get a good 20 minutes a day extra.

Doing the Washing

With laundry, you may decide to carry on regardless, providing they know how to use the washing machine in an emergency, that is, when you haven't washed the outfit which has been hiding at the back of the wardrobe for weeks, the one you *knew* was the *only* thing they could possibly wear that night. Otherwise, whoever's in charge automatically gives their clothing priority, and when it comes to underpinnings in a mixed sex household, there's liable to be some embarrassment. They can still put washed clothes on the line or the airer, and gather it in, folded neatly, to go in the airing cupboard. They may even rescue it from the garden when it starts raining, instead of completely failing to recognize that the one event necessitates the other.

Shopping

Ask them to check with you whether shopping is required whenever they go out; without a car, special trips are necessary for items like soap powder, and stocking up for bank holidays. Again, if you do half the trips, mistaken purchases can usually be redeemed, but most children enjoy this job when left to choose certain items, from bath oil to packets of biscuits. They see for themselves how much things cost (especially with the occasional worry about whether they have enough money) and understand the situation better than from your complaints about the price of noodles. They're also more likely to be interested in learning to cook when allowed a choice of menu, rather than following your suggestions. And now and again, forgo the evening meal for something from the chippie. It may not be altogether sensible, health- and pocket-wise, but doesn't cost much more than the average convenience meal, and makes a pleasant change, especially since the washing-up can be dispensed with.

Examining your list of chores is a good step to improve timekeeping. Some daily jobs could be done every other day, or weekly tasks could be spaced ten days apart or maybe put on a fortnightly basis? A few days extra between the more occasional jobs also adds up, to give you more time to yourself.

30

Part-time Work

The Benefits of Working

Having repeatedly done your sums, tried everything else to get the money you need, there's nothing else for it; you have to get a job. You are not the only one, and competition is part of the problem. But it's not just a question of having extra cash (one way of saving money is being too busy to spend it). Once you start working, it's proof of your CV: you are diligent, organized, reliable and able to use your initiative. Plus, you have extra experience. Golden opportunities don't always coincide with ample funds, and you don't want to be in a position where you have to turn down something you really want, simply because you can't afford it. If you think you will need to look for work eventually, don't leave it too long. In areas where there is high unemployment, you'll be up against people with a more flexible timetable and fewer commitments.

Looking for Work

There's quite a high turnover with part-timers, and if you are determined to find work, you usually succeed, particularly when prepared to tackle anything, within reason: shops, supermarkets, restaurants, clubs, pubs, bars, offices. If there's nothing you fancy advertised in the jobcentre or the local papers, ask around. Not all job vacancies are made public because first, they won't go begging for long and second, it saves the business being inundated with enquiries. Even if you are just added to a local store's waiting list, you still stand a chance; increase the possibilities by getting your name on as many waiting lists as possible. But remove your name once you have got work elsewhere; if you work part-time, there's no point antagonizing somebody who may be a future employer.

Register with a temping agency if you have suitable skills, such as word processing or market research. It may not ensure regular employment, but could keep you solvent and give you more experience of working in different fields, perhaps making some useful contacts to enhance future prospects. No matter how desperate for work, think twice before you go in for anything that looks at all dodgy. Clinical testing, for example, can mean plenty of money and takes up little time but undergoing medical trials is a risky business. Double-check with your own doctor first.

Once at the point where you realize that you have got to get a job – desperation – even if you're prepared to do anything, make a few notes first. See those suggested in Chapter 21. List the things you enjoy, and include everything you can think of, no matter how trivial. Next, list what you hate doing (hopefully, a bit shorter). Third, list everything you are good at. Finally, make a list of any jobs advertised which have possibilities, divided into work which is done outdoors and work indoors, including the most convenient of all: work carried out in your own home.

Problems with Working Part-time

Part-time work gives you longer to spend with your children, but there are several disadvantages compared with full-time work. Wages are often low and you're unlikely to be entitled to the same benefits such as sick leave, holidays and so on. Set hours make it easier for you to arrange a suitable routine, but working shifts can cause problems with organizing childcare, although it may give you more time with your children. Flexitime sometimes makes life easier, although it depends whether childcare provision can accommodate your starting work early or finishing late. With qualifications and experience, one possibility is job-sharing: working half days, half a week or alternate weeks. This can be arranged by the employer, or you could suggest it. Then advertise or ask around; if you have a friend with children the same age, you could work together.

Even a part-time job can mean massive upheaval, but you could ease yourself back in by doing some voluntary work. You're unlikely to get paid but helping others can be salutary, not least when their problems help take your mind off your own. You also get used to mixing with people; for example, dealing with customers if you help out in a charity shop.

Organizing Yourself

Once you are actually employed, you'll inevitably suffer from weariness, partly due to worrying about starting work again, so it should wear off as you settle down. Work is often stressful but those problems should be confined to the workplace and not brought home, and vice versa. When working alongside other parents, get to know them and find out how they learned to cope, especially with worrying about the children and how they will manage without you. If you have to work because you need the money, it's pointless feeling guilty about it. There again, few women can afford to stay home, but why feel guilty if you're working because you want to? It's other people's opinions which make any justification necessary.

Organize yourself to cover as many eventualities as possible, allowing plenty of time to sort the children out, and to get to work and home again. Make contingency plans for any crises, like sudden illnesses, but don't fret about things which could go wrong. They will, but rarely to the extent pictured. And don't let your imagination run away with being petrified about going back to work; once you've managed to get a job, your employer clearly thinks you're capable. If lack of self-confidence keeps nagging you, see what courses are available. Something related to your work will help, or training to be more assertive; learning the basics of psychology shows you how to put things into perspective. Concentrate on the positive aspects of going out to work, not just financial gain. A job helps make you independent and helps give you a sense of worth, especially once you begin to make progress. It raises your status in the eyes of your children, family and friends, and broadens your social circle, while your children benefit by having more dealings with other adults and children and learning to be more self-reliant.

31

Future Prospects

As a single parent and working mother who also makes some time for herself, where does your future lie?

Women at Home

Parents have always been anxious about their children's prospects, though now it's not so much wanting them to do better than they did, more hoping they don't end up worse off. Work is seen as essential for providing money, stability and financial independence, and the children of working parents are capable of understanding the positive aspects. They are often high achievers themselves. However, some working mothers consider that time spent with children at home must always be filled with activities, although it's the emotional bond between parent and child which is more important. They may not even expect children to help round the house because any conflict eats up quality time. But with most families being smaller nowadays, children actually receive more attention than in the 1960s.

Parents at Work and at Home

Life at work and at home would improve with better childcare; for example, if employees were allowed a few family days to allow for emergencies, in addition to sick/holiday leave. Or if facilities included some form of insurance, with a paid-for, reliable, back-up service. Fortunately, more employers are implementing family-friendly policies and one of the simplest solutions is a flexible working pattern. Fewer worries about childcare means parents can concentrate more on their jobs. People who are more content with their lives work much better, which should keep their employers happier (and better off).

Women tend to do umpteen things at once, which is not a natural talent in men, though house-husbands often develop a close bond with their children because they get undivided attention. In the USA, only 7 per cent are traditional households (Mom at home, Dad in the office), with the fastest increase in families headed by a single father. Many husbands are opting for role reversal in order to be with their children (five TV sitcoms feature single dads), although they have discovered one big disadvantage: fathers who choose to stay at home are regarded with distrust. Similarly, society undervalues stay-at-home mothers, although managers in America congratulate pregnant women who leave on 'their promotion' (you can just picture the card).

In the UK, childless women are pitied, while mothers are all but invisible until their children play up, when they come in for criticism. Children are still not made welcome everywhere, and are even resented for spoiling everybody else's enjoyment. Just 20 per cent of trains have facilities for changing nappies or breastfeeding; 5 per cent of stations. About half of those over 45 agree with full parental leave for men, while three-quarters of 16- to 34-year-olds think it's a good idea, men (61 per cent) and women (69 per cent) for once almost in agreement. Women executives who give up work for their children are deplored by feminists because it proves to men that women cannot handle top jobs.

Women at Work

Thirty-seven per cent of working women think single parents should be expected to go back to work, yet 70 per cent would choose to stay at home if money were no object. The average family needs £19,000 per year to manage and the average wage is £17,000. More than half of mothers would like to continue their career part time, as a job share, and 81 per cent think women have too many roles and are overworked. In 21 per cent of households, nobody has a job; in 25 per cent, just the husband; whereas in 62 per cent of families, both parents work. One in six mothers with children under four works full time, increasing to nearly 50 per cent of mothers who have under-fives, and 71 per cent, where the youngest is aged five to ten years. As for encouraging women to get jobs, since the care sector is a fast growing area, most of them will be working in childcare, suggesting a ready-made motto for the government: *quis custodiet custodes?*

Women's Place at Work

About one-third of retail businesses in 1997 were set up by women, and in a survey for the eightieth anniversary of International Women's Day, over three-quarters thought their educational opportunities had improved; hence greater access to good jobs (although that depends on who was being asked). As more women have become better educated, they start work in their mid-twenties rather than in their late teens. Forty per cent of professionals are women, but high-powered jobs mean long hours, which are hard on families. Though women outnumber men in the workplace, they earn about 80 per cent of men's average hourly wage, and are dissatisfied because of men's attitude at work, resulting in thousands of cases of sexual harassment and discrimination. Men often object when there are codes of practice and behaviour to ensure positive discrimination, and can be very hostile towards women, especially bosses. Some believe menial jobs should be left to women, even in companies which arrange training (from schools onwards) and crèches and insist women and men be treated equally.

Little girls may still play at being brides but young women are learning to be more assertive than in the past. They aim for job satisfaction and personal fulfilment but, increasingly, need security while men want more material rewards – rises and promotion. When men lose their jobs, they expect to go in for something of equal value, and refuse to consider anything which seems like taking a step backward, even temporarily. Women are more flexible and will have a go at anything in the hope it will lead somewhere, knowing it's more sensible to be doing something, and better for your self-esteem.

There is much doom and gloom concerning women's career prospects because few can have 100 per cent success with motherhood, marriage and the managing director's job. Work has come in for criticism because of the need for changes in the market and on the part of men, and also because it is seen as an end in itself. Man or woman, you are expected to be fully committed to your job, even at the expense of your personal life and family. Men are often criticized because they seem to be prepared to do this, although they probably feel that they have no other choice.

As an employee, one priority should be flexible working practices. Check the company's policy and whether it varies in different departments. If not, but if they are open to the idea in principle, some research should help convince them of the benefits in terms of savings, time-management and manpower. If you need to approach your boss on the subject and you're a member of a trade union, speak to your local organizer first. Your proposal should be thoroughly prepared in advance, with the details down on paper, emphasizing the benefits to the employer: greater commitment from existing employees; more effective output (since flexibility means improved time-management); reduced loss of experienced employees if they need to change their hours, hence less need to incur costs with recruitment and training; more flexibility attracts more prospective employees.

Time to Work

Check how any changes affect you: pay, holidays, employment rights, pension. Is this a short-term arrangement or long-term? With the latter, it needs reviewing after a set period. This should be agreed upon from the start to help allay worries about your future prospects. What is most suitable for your home life as well as your job? Would you have the opportunity later to do full-time work? Flexitime has proved very successful. With short lunch breaks, you can start or leave later or earlier, and any hours saved used to cover time off to look after sick children. Similarly, compressed hours means working longer in a day but fewer days each week. V-time, which originated in the USA, allows you to work for a reduced length of time over an agreed period; term-time working involves taking unpaid leave during school holidays, although your pay may be spread to cover the whole year.

Job-sharing has proved popular, with two people taking it in turns. Many parents opt for jobs which can be done during school hours or part-time but these tend to be poorly paid by comparison. You could end up doing enough work for it to be classified as full-time, without the remuneration. Working from home, usually in clerical and professional jobs, is becoming more popular, though it's easier when you have older children rather than a baby.

Education

The future seems to be lifelong learning, that is, training for work at several stages of life rather than acquiring knowledge for the sake of it. Currently, companies tend to do more teaching than educational establishments such as universities, largely because conventional education is for the purpose of passing exams and gaining awards. It needs to be much wider: identifying appropriate skills, the right age to learn them, how to apply them and the various levels of ability. This would help individuals to adapt to the changing world and education, like the workplace, will change, leading to an information society.

Life is full of change and all kinds of opportunities. Whatever it holds for you, once you have succeeded as a single parent, you know you are capable of making a success of anything else.

Useful Addresses

Self

Bereavement

Bereavement Trust
Stanford Hall
Loughborough
Leics LE12 5QR
Telephone: 01509 852333

Provides information about support services nationwide.

Cruse – Bereavement Care
Director, Rosemary Pearce
Cruse House, 126 Sheen Road
Richmond
Surrey TW9 1UR
Telephone: 0181 940 4818
Bereavement line: 0181 332 7227

Two hundred branches nationwide. Publications include help for bereaved children (including fiction and books for those with learning disabilities), counselling and resource packs for professionals, including schools.

The Lesbian and Gay Bereavement Project
Colindale House
Colindale Avenue
London NW9
Telephone helpline: 0181 455 8894 (24 hours)

Provides contacts throughout the country.

National Association of Widows/
Widowers Advisory Trust
54–57 Allison Street
Digbeth
Birmingham B5 5TH
Telephone: 0121 643 8348

Contacts

National Federation of 18 plus Groups
Head Office, Nicholson House
Old Court Road
Newent, Glos.
GL18 1AG
Telephone: 01531 821210

Groups nationwide, providing a wide range of activities for 18 to 30s.

National Federation of Solo Clubs
Room 8, Ruskin Chambers
191 Corporation Street
Birmingham B4 6RY
Telephone: 0121 236 2879

One hundred branches nationwide, open to single, widowed, divorced and separated people aged 25 to 65.

Pen Pal and Correspondence Clubs

NB: When writing, SAEs must always be enclosed

Expansions Unlimited
Christine Michael
Box No 30 South PDO
Nottingham NG2 7JP
Telephone: 0115 981 9397
Fax: 0115 982 6839

Mates
Sue Godfrey
222 Canal Cottage
Pool Road
Burntwood
Walsall
Staffs WS7 8QW

Singlescape
18 Woolvestone Close
Suffolk IP2 9RY

Largest UK penfriend group, offering support and self-help.

Leisure Activities/Networks (Information Services)

CLAN
Telephone: 0181 904 8120

London-based, events range from pub lunches to theatre outings. Chairman Linda Greenbury is the author of *Portable Careers: Surviving Your Partner's Relocation* and *Jobs for the Over 50s*. Trial membership available.

NEXUS Information Service
Nexus House
6 The Quay
Bideford
North Devon EX39 2HW
Telephone: 01237 471704/421619

SPICE The Adventure Group (Special Programme of Initiative, Challenge and Excitement)
13 Thorpe Street
Manchester
M16 9PR
Telephone: 0161 872 2213

Nine regional groups offering a wide range of activities.

Women's Groups

Single Again
FREEPOST
LON 3735
London W4 4BR
Telephone: 0181 749 3745

Provides a regular bulletin and special offers on products and services, advice lines and information pack; publishes quarterly magazine *Single Again*.

National Alliance of Women's Organizations
37 Hatton Gardens
London EC1N 8EB
Telephone: 0171 242 0878

National Association of Women's Clubs
5 Vernon Rise
London WC1X 9EP
Telephone: 0171 837 1434

National Women's Register
3A Vulcan House, Vulcan Road
Norwich NR6 6AQ
Telephone: 01603 406767

Counselling and Support Groups

Bullying

Anti-Bullying Campaign
6 Borough High Street
London SE1 9QQ
Telephone: 0171 378 1446

Fact sheet available.

National Association of Victim Support Schemes
Cranmer House
39 Brixton Road
London SW9 6DZ
Telephone: 0171 735 9166

Local branches and specialist workers in most areas, providing emotional support, practical advice and information.

Domestic Violence

Women's Aid Federation
PO Box 391
Bristol BS99 7WS
Telephone: 0345 023468 (national helpline Mon. to Thurs. 10 a.m. to 5 p.m., Fri. and Sat. 10 a.m. to 3 p.m.)

Children

Cry-sis
BM Cry-sis
London WC1N 3XX
Telephone: 0171 404 5011

Support for families with children who are excessively demanding.

Family Rights Group
The Print House
18 Ashwin Street
London E8 3DL
Telephone. 0171 249 0008 (Advice), 0171 923 2628 (Enquiries)

Offers practical and legal advice, especially about local authority care.

National Children's Bureau
8 Wakeley Street
London EC1V 7QE
Telephone: 0171 843 6000

National Society for the Prevention of Cruelty to Children (NSPCC)
42 Curtain Road
London CC2A 3NH
Telephone: 0171 825 2500
Child protection helpline:
0800 800500 (24 hours)

Offers information and advice about children's welfare.

Relationships

Relate
Herbert Gray College
Little Church Street
Rugby
Warks CV21 3AP

Local branches; can also be used by unmarried couples.

General

British Association for Counselling
1 Regent Place
Rugby
Warks CV21 2PJ
Telephone: 01788 578328

Samaritans
24-hour confidential helpline at head office: 01753 532713

Local number – see front of phone book.

Finances

The Child Poverty Action Group
1–5 Bath Street
London EC1V 9PY
Telephone: 0171 253 3406

Publications include *The National Welfare Benefits Handbook*.

Benefits

Disability benefits free advice line:
0800 882200
Income Support
See under Benefits Agency in phone book

Child Benefit and One-parent Benefit
Child Benefit Centre, DSS
Washington
Newcastle upon Tyne NE88 1AA

Family Credit Unit
DSS, Government Buildings
Cop Lane
Penwortham
Preston PR1 0SA
Family Credit Helpline:
01253 500050
Free line: 0800 500222

Housing and Council Tax Benefit

Ring the switchboard of your local authority; address and phone number in *Yellow Pages*, under Local Government.

Debt

National Debtline
318 Summer Lane
Birmingham B19 3RL
Telephone: 0121 359 8501

Maintenance

Child Support Agency
Millbank Tower
21–24 Millbank
London SW1 4QU
Telephone (advice line): 0345 133133

Health

Health Information Service
Telephone: 0800 665544

Free confidential information service for both individual enquiries about health and details about local health services.

Healthwise Freepost (LV 6535)
Liverpool L1 4BW

Helpline open 9 a.m. to 9 p.m. every day of the year: 0800 665544

National Association for Mental Health (MIND)
Granta House
15–19 Broadway
Stratford
London E15 4BQ
Telephone: 0181 519 2122
Information and services, including leaflets, about a range of health problems.

Disability

Contact-a-family
70 Tottenham Court Road
London W1P 0HA
Helpline: 0171 383 3555

National charity; information and support for families with children with special needs.

Disability Alliance (ERA)
1st Floor East, Universal House
88–94 Wentworth Street
London E1 7SA
Telephone: 0171 247 8776

Parentability c/o National Childbirth Trust
Alexander House
Oldham Terrace
London W3 6NH
Telephone: 0181 992 8637

Advice and support for parents with disabilities.

Housing

Shelter (National Campaign for Homeless People)
88 Old Street
London EC1V 9HU
Telephone: 0171 505 2000

Can also provide details of local housing advice centres.

Legal Services

Children

Children's Legal Centre
c/o University of Essex
Wivenhoe Park
Colchester CO4 3SQ
Telephone: 01206 872466 (Admin.)
Advice Line: 01206 873820 (Mon. to
Fri. 2 p.m. to 5 p.m.)

Advice on the law and young people.

Disability

Disability Law Service
49 Bedford Row
London WC1R 4LR
Telephone: 0171 831 80931 (free
service)

Family

Solicitors' Family Law
 Association (SFLA)
PO Box 302
Orpington
Kent BR6 8QX
Telephone: 01689 850227

Send SAE for list of local members.

Gay and Lesbian

Gay and Lesbian Legal Advice
 (GLAD)
Telephone: 0171 837 5212 (free advice
line Mon. to Thurs. 7 p.m. to 9.30 p.m.)

Lesbian and Gay Switchboard
PO Box 7324, London N1
Telephone: 0171 837 7324

Details of local support groups.

Women

Rights of Women
52–54 Featherstone Street
London EC1 8RT
Telephone: 0171 251 6577

Free advice by telephone.

Single-parent Organizations

Gingerbread
16–17 Clerkenwell Close
London EC1R 0AA
Telephone: 0171 336 8183
Advice line: 0171 336 8184

Self-help association with about 400
groups in the UK, plus branches in
Northern Ireland, Scotland and Wales.
Regular meetings to provide help and
support for parents and children, often
with a range of social activities. Also
provides training opportunities for those
seeking work, and a range of publications: advice leaflets, newsletters (including one for children), reports, guides and
packs. Membership per year: £10.

Home-start Schemes
2 Salisbury Road
Leics LE1 7QR
Telephone: 0116 233 9955

Celebrating its Silver Jubilee, the char-
itable trust is 'investing in families',
having been established with the aim of
helping young families under stress,
that is, any family with at least one
child under five years. There are now
over 200 schemes nationwide, with
over 5,000 trained volunteers who will
visit one or more families each week,
providing friendship, advice and support. The scheme organizers also run
group meetings and social events.

National Council for One Parent
  Families
255 Kentish Town Road
London NW5 2LX
Telephone: 0171 267 1361

Acts on behalf of single parents, providing advice, information and support. Membership per year: £5.

SPAN (Single Parent Action Network)
Millpond, Baptist Street
Easton
Bristol BS5 0YW
Telephone: 0171 951 4231
E-mail:
annie@spanuk.demon.co.uk

A multiracial group of single parents working to improve the lives of one-parent families in the UK and Europe. Provides information (newsletter) and support and runs workshops, meetings and conferences. Allocates starter grants to help set up single-parent groups. Free membership for those with an income of less than £10,000 a year; £15 per year for those receiving £10,000 to £100,000.

Single-parent Fathers

Families Need Fathers
134 Curtain Road
London EC2A 3AR
Telephone: 0171 613 5060
Helpline: 0181 886 0970

National network offering advice and support.

Children

Bullying

Anti-Bullying Campaign
10 Borough High Street
London SE1 9QQ
Telephone: 0171 378 1446

Fact sheet available.

Kidscape
152 Buckingham Palace Road
London SW1W 9TR
Telephone: 0171 730 3300

The No Blame Approach
Lucky Duck Publishing & Enterprises
34 Wellington Park
Clifton
Bristol BS8 2UW
Telephone: 0117 973 2882

Courses, packs, videos, etc., mostly aimed at schools but very useful for parents.

Counselling

Childline
Freepost 1111
London W1 0BR
Telephone: 0800 1111 (24 hours)

The Young Minds Trust
22a Boston Place
London NW1 6ER
Telephone: 0171 247262

Education

National Association for Gifted
  Children (NAGC)
540 Elder Gate
Milton Keynes MK9 1LR
Telephone: 01908 673677

Home Education

Education Otherwise
PO Box 7420
London N9 9SG
Telephone: 0171 0891 518 303

Family and Educational
  Helpline UK
105 Links Road
Tooting
London SW17 9EJ
Telephone (helpline): 0181 696 9970

The Parenting Eucation and Support
  Forum
8 Wakeley Street
London EC1V 7QE
Telephone: 0171 843 6009

Mediation

Divorce Conciliation and
  Advisory Service (DCAS)
38 Ebury Street
London SW1W 0LU
Telephone: 0171 730 2422

Help and advice for arranging joint
care of children.

National Family Mediation
9 Tavistock Place
London WC1H 9SN
Telephone: 0171 383 5993

Details of mediation services nationwide.

Parenting

Association of Shared Parenting
PO Box 2000
Dudley
West Midlands DY1 IY2

Support for parents to encourage the
child's right to nurture from both
parents.

Both Parents Forever
39 Clonmore Avenue
Orpington
Kent BR6 9LE
Telephone: 01689 854343

Promotes rights of children, parents
and grandparents. Offers help in child
abduction cases.

Exploring Parenthood
4 Ivory Place
Treadgold Street
London W11 4BP
Telephone: 0171 221 4471
Fax: 0171 221 5501
Advice line: 0171 221 66812
(10 a.m. to 4 p.m. Mon. to Fri.)

Advice, education, information and
counselling for parents; wide range of
useful fact sheets including: divorce
and children; step-parenting; the working parent. Holds conferences and
workshops, plus monthly meetings for
isolated parents and children at the
Sunday Centre. Runs the Moyenda
Project (Black and Asian families).

Families for Freedom
c/o the Worldwrite Centre
14 Theobald's Road
London WC1X 8PF
Telephone: 0171 254 1389
(Tiffany Jenkins)

Offers fact sheets on various aspects of
parenting, campaigning for fairer treatment of families.

The Family Welfare Association
501–505 Kingsland Road
London E8 4AU
Telephone: 0171 254 6251

A variety of services offered to people
facing social and emotional difficulties
(bereavement, homelessness, poverty,
etc.).

The New Learning Centre
211 Sumatra Road
London NW6 1PF
Telephone: 0171 794 0321

Runs parenting courses

Parent-Link
Telephone: 0171 485 8535

Operates self-help groups run by parents, usually two-hour sessions for a 13-week period. Fees vary, according to circumstances.

Parent Network
Room 2, Winchester House
Kennington Park
11 Cranmore Road
London SW9 1EJ
Telephone: 0171 735 1214

Nationwide groups, providing training and practical help on parenting.

Parentline
Helpline: 01702 559900
(Mon. to Fri. 9 a.m. to 6 p.m.)

Offers support and advice.

Parents Anonymous
Helpline: 0171 263 8918; 0181 689 3136

Stepfamilies

National Stepfamily Association
Chapel House
18 Hatton Place
London EC1N 8RU
Telephone: 0171 209 2460

Support, advice and information; newsletters.

Teenagers

Brook Advisory Centre
Tottenham Court Road Centre
233 Tottenham Court Road
London W1P 9AE
Telephone: 0171 580 2991

Information Shops for Young People:
National Youth Agency
Telephone: 0116 2856789

Quindo Centre
2 West Drive
London NW11 7QH
Telephone: 0181 455 8698

Stand Your Ground courses.

The Trust for the Study of
    Adolescence (TSA)
23 New Road
Brighton
East Sussex BN1 1WZ
Telephone: 01273 693311
Fax: 01273 679907

Also arrange conferences (counselling adolescents; eating disorders, and so on) and offer board games: 'Discoveries' (Self-realization and awareness of others, age 15+): £26.

Youth Access
1a Taylor's Yard
67 Alderbrook Road
London SW12 8AD
Telephone: 0181 772 9900

For youth advice and counselling sources.

Holidays

Holiday Care Service
2nd Floor, Imperial Buildings
Victoria Road
Horley
Surrey RH6 7PZ
Telephone: 01293 774535

Guide to holidays for one-parent families available.

HELP – Holiday Endeavour for
Lone Parents
57 Owston Road
Doncaster DN6 8DA
Telephone: 01302 728791

Holidays One Parents (HOP)
51 Hampshire Road
Droylsdon
Manchester M43 7PL
Telephone: 0161 370 0337 (coordina-
tor Bill Softley)

Organizes low-cost holidays and runs a
national befriending service.

Single Parent Travel Club
811 Cliff Road
Wooldale
Holmfirth
West Yorkshire
HD7 1YP
Telephone: 01484 688143 (6 p.m. to 8
p.m.)

Also provides advice and support, plus
information about social events; quarterly newsletters.

Work

Childcare

Daycare Trust/National
  Childcare Campaign
Wesley House
4 Wild Court
London WC2B 4AU
Telephone: 0171 405 5617

Kids' Club Network
3 Muirfield Crescent
London E14 9SZ
Telephone: 0171 512 2100

National body for out-of-school childcare for children aged 5 to 12.

National Association of Toy and
  Leisure Libraries
68 Churchway
London NW1 1LT
Telephone: 0171 387 9592

National Childminding
  Association
8 Mason Hill
Bromley
Kent BR2 9EY
Telephone: 0181 464 6164

The National Early Years Network
77 Holloway Road
London N7 8JZ
Telephone: 0171 607 9573

For details of local services for under-
eights.

The Parent Helpline
Telephone: 0171 837 5513
(10 a.m. to 5 p.m.)

Local childcare information.

Playpen
Telephone: 0171 224 6603

Pressure group calling for introduction
of a national register for nannies.

Pre-School Learning Alliance
61/63 Kings Cross Road
London WC1X 9LL
Telephone: 0171 833 0991

Information about voluntarily run UK
playgroups.

Continuing Education

National Extension College
18 Brooklands Avenue
Cambridge CB2 2HN
Telephone: 01223 31664

Correspondence courses; wide range
of subjects.

The Open College
FREEPOST TK1006
Brentford
Middlesex TW8 8BR
Freephone: 0800 300760

Courses include retraining and updating skills.

Open University (OU)
Enquiry Office
PO Box 71
Milton Keynes MK7 6AG
Telephone: 01908 274066

Vocational, non-degree and degree courses.

Work

National Association of
  Volunteer Bureaux
New Oxford House
Waterloo Street
Birmingham B2 5UG
Telephone: 0121 633 4555

New Ways to Work
309 Upper Street
London N1 2TY
Telephone: 0171 226 4026
Enquiries: Tues. 10 a.m. to 1 p.m.;
Wed. 12 noon to 3 p.m.

Booklets and fact sheets on job-sharing.

Parents at Work
45 Beech Street
Barbican
London EC2Y 8AD
Telephone: 0171 628 3578
Special Needs Helpline: 0171 588 0802

The voice of working parents. Campaigns to improve the quality of life for working parents and their children, including single parents. Regular newsletters, variety of fact sheets and publications, etc. available. Membership: £18; £12 for low-income families.

The Women Returners' Network
100 Park Village East
London NW1 3SR
(Information Officer: Gill Heath)
Telephone: 0171 468 2290/1/2

Runs conferences, events and workshops. Quarterly newsletter, information sheets, helpline, etc. available. Membership per year: £10.

Further Reading

NCOPF Publications

Benefits/Tax
Children: Legal rights and responsibilities of parents not living together
Getting Through: A lone parent's guide to gaining the best help and advice
Holidays
Housing
Maintenance and the Child Support Agency
Returning to work: A guide for lone parents
Single and Pregnant
Splitting up: Divorce and unmarried relationship breakdown
What to Do after the Death of a Partner

Bereavement

Paul Harris, *What to do when Someone Dies*, Which? Consumer Guide, Penguin, London, 1998.
Sylvia Murphy, *Dealing with a Death in the Family*, How To Books, Oxford, 1996.

Cookery

Cas Clarke, *Peckish But Poor*, Headline, London, 1993.
Cassandra Kent, *The Ultimate Book of Cookery Hints and Tips*, Dorling Kindersley, London, 1997.
Alastair Williams, *The Student Grub Guide*, and *The Vegetarian Student Grub Guide*, Summersdale, Chichester, 1997.

DIY and Repairs

Cassandra Kent, *The Ultimate Book of Household Hints and Tips*, Dorling Kindersley, London, 1996.
John McGowan and Roger DuBern, DK Pocket Encyclopaedias: *Home Decorating, Home Repair*, Dorling Kindersley, London, 1991.

Finance

Benefits

Martin Rathfelder, *How to Claim State Benefits*, How To Books, 3rd edition, Oxford, 1995.

Debt

Mike Woolfe and Jill Ivison, *Debt Advice Handbook*, CPAG.

Economizing

Richard Benson, *How to Save Money*, Summersdale Tip-Top Guides, 1995.

Jane Furnival, *Mr Thrifty's How to Save Money on Absolutely Everything*, Pan Books, London, 1994.

Students

Louise Clarke, *Cosmopolitan Guide to Student Life*, Penguin, London, 1996.

Gwenda Thomas, *Students' Money Matters*, Trotman (supported by UCAS), London, 1996.

General

Leo Gough, *Managing Your Money*, Hodder & Stoughton Teach Yourself Books, London, 1996.

Jonquil Lowe, *Be Your Own Financial Adviser*, Which? Consumer Guide, Penguin, London, 1996.

Health

Adults

Denise Brown, *Massage*, Hodder & Stoughton Teach Yourself Books, London, 1997.

Cathy Hopkins, *101 Short Cuts to Relaxation*, Bloomsbury, London, 1997.

Terry Looker and Olga Gregson, *Managing Stress*, Hodder & Stoughton Teach Yourself Books, London, 1997.

Joan Radford, *The Complete Book of Family Aromatherapy*, Foulsham, Berkshire, 1993.

Maxine Tobias and John Patrick Sullivan, *The Complete Stretching Book*, Dorling Kindersley, London, 1997.

Children

Carole Baldock, *Teenage Pregnancy I: Making the Choices; II: Having the Baby*, Knight & Bishop, Huddersfield, 1996.

Claire Beeken with Rosanna Greenstreet, *My Body, My Enemy: My Thirteen Year Battle with Anorexia Nervosa*, Thorsons, London, 1997.

Pamela De Salvo and Tricia Skuse, *The Really Helpful Directory: Services for Pregnant Teenagers and Young Parents*, TSA Publishing Ltd, Brighton, 1993.

Dr Frances Peck, *Handbook for Young Mothers*, Rainer Foundation, London, 1993.

NB: This is available free at some clinics or agencies.

Psychology

Dr Susan Forward with Donna Frazier, *Emotional Blackmail*, Bantam Press, London, 1997.

Lillian Glass, *Attracting Terrific People*, Thorsons, London, 1998.

Thomas A. Harris, MD, *I'm OK – You're OK*, Pan, London, 1973.

Alan Houel with Christian Godefroy, *How to Cope with Difficult People*, Sheldon Press, London, 1997.

James W. Jones, *In the Middle of This Road We Call Our Life*, Thorsons, London, 1995.

M. Peck, *The Road Less Travelled*, Arrow, London, 1978.

Relationships

Christina Basciano, *Relationship Breakdown: A Survival Guide*, Ward Lock, London, 1997.

Helen Garlick, *The Which? Guide to Divorce*, Penguin, London.

Elizabeth Mapstone, *War of Words: Women and Men Arguing*, Chatto & Windus, London, 1998.

Roy van de Brink-Budgen, *How to Survive Divorce*, How To Books, 2nd edition, Oxford, 1994.

Other

The Joseph Rowntree Foundation produces reports which include topics such as: *Managing on a Low Income*; *Diets of Lone-parent Families*; *Setting up Home as a Young Single Mother*. The Homestead, 40 Water End, York YO3 6LP. Telephone: 01904 620072.

Family Policy Studies Centre, 231 Baker Street, London NW1 6XE. Telephone: 0171 486 8211. Recent publications: *Single Lone Mothers: Problems, Prospects and Policies*; *The Employment of Lone Parents: A Comparison of Policy in Twenty Countries*.

Children

Bereavement

Rosemary Wells, *Helping Children Cope with Grief*, Sheldon Press, London, 1988.

Divorce

Anne Charlish, *Caught in the Middle: Helping Children to Cope with Separation and Divorce*, Ward Lock, London, 1997.

Rosemary Wells, *Helping Children Cope with Divorce*, Sheldon Press, London, 1997.

Parenting

Carol Baker, *Getting on with Your Children*, Longman, London, 1990.

Michele Elliott, *A Practical Guide to Talking with Children*, Hodder & Stoughton, London, 1988.

Even Better Parents, Lucky Duck Publishing, Bristol, 1997. Training pack, video, manual, etc.

Brenda Houghton, *The Good Child: How to Instil a Sense of Right and Wrong in Your Child*, Headline, London, 1998.

Clare Shaw, *The 5-Minute Mum: Time Management for Busy Parents*, Hodder & Stoughton Positive Parenting series, London, 1995.

Dr Stanley Turecki with Leslie Tonner, *The Difficult Child: How to Understand and Cope with Your Temperamental 2–6 year old*, Piatkus, London, 1995.

Bullying

Carole Baldock, *Bullying*, Knight & Bishop, Huddersfield, 1997.

Michele Elliott, *101 Ways to Deal with Bullying*, Hodder & Stoughton, London, 1997.

Sarah Lawson, *Helping Children Cope with Bullying*, Sheldon Press, London, 1995.

Dr John Pearce, *Fighting, Teasing and Bullying*, Thorsons, London, 1989.

George Robinson and Barbara Maines, *Crying for Help*, Lucky Duck Publishing, Bristol, 1997.

Education

Ken Adams, *Bring out the Genius in Your Child*, Ward Lock, London, 1997.

Carole Baldock, *Aiming for As: From GCSE to A level*, Knight & Bishop, Huddersfield, 1998.

Jennie and Lance Lindon, *Help Your Child Through School*, Hodder & Stoughton, London, 1994.

Teenagers

Helen Braid, ed., *A Stranger at My Table: Women Write about Mothering Adolescents*, The Women's Press, London, 1997.

Elizabeth Fenwick and Dr Tony Smith, *Adolescence: The Survival Guide for Parents and Teenagers*, Dorling Kindersley, London, 1993.

Debi Roker and John Coleman, *Teenagers in the Family*, Hodder & Stoughton, London, 1995.

Paul van Heeswyk, *Analysing Adolescence*, Sheldon Press, London, 1997.

Resource Packs

The Guide Association and The Body Shop, *Girls Get Real!* Self-esteem activity pack. Fiona Aitken, Youth Programme Manager, The Guide Association, 17–19 Buckingham Palace Road, London SW1W 0PT.

Adrienne Katz, *Understanding Our Daughters*, Exploring Parenthood, 4 Ivory Place, Treadgold Street, London W11 4BP. Telephone: 0171 221 4471.

Working Abroad

Godfrey Golzen, *Working Abroad: The Daily Telegraph Guide to Working and Living Abroad*, Trotman, 1996.

Mark Hempshell, *How To Do Voluntary Work Abroad*, How To Books, Oxford, 1995.

Nick Vandome, *Spending a Year Abroad: How to Have the Time of Your Life Anywhere Around the World*, How To Books, Oxford, 1996.

Books for Children

Judy Bastyra, *Kid's Guide to Making Money and Keeping It!* Bloomsbury, London, 1997.

Karen Bryant-Mole, *Splitting Up* and *Step Families*, Wayland, London, 1994.

Work

Job Applications

Compiled by Lee Jarvis, *Classic Sample Letters: Letters that Get Results and Have Stood the Test of Time*, Foulsham, Berkshire, 1997.

Time-management

Sally Garratt, *Manage Your Time*, HarperCollins, London, 1994.

Eileen Gillibrand and Jenny Mosley, *When I Go to Work, I Feel Guilty*, Thorsons, London, 1997.

Elizabeth Perle McKenna, *When Work Doesn't Work Anymore*, Simon & Schuster, London, 1997.

Working from Home

Ian Phillipson, *How to Work from Home*, How To Books, 2nd edition, Oxford, 1995.

Index

bereavement: death of partner, widows/widowers 4–5

childcare 106–11; childminders' nannies, nurseries 52–7
children: education 56–8; health 62–5; jobs 75–7; leisure 59–61; pocket money 60; special needs 37, 53, 70, 94; teenagers 66–8: teenagers: education 56–8; health 63–4; jobs 72–7

divorce: attitudes towards 1–3, 7–13; effects of 47–51

education 55–9; computers, using 98–100; further education 95–7, 111–12; skills, acquiring 85–90
employment: careers 78–81; part-time 105–7; working from home 78–9, 108–9; working parents 78–9, 108–12

finances (form filling): child benefit 28–30; council tax, housing 28–9; CSA 29–30; Family Credit 25–6; health costs 27–8; student grants 92–4; Income Support 27; Income Tax 91–2; National

Insurance 92

health 17–19: exercise 17–18
health problems 20–2: anxiety and depression, stress 20–2; eating disorders 18–19; sex education 63–4; teenage pregnancy 1–2, 63–4
holidays 69–71
household: clothing 36, 42–3; DIY and repairs 35–7; food 39–41; housework 101–4

leisure: activities, hobbies, interests 44–6; pets, keeping 61

money: bills, budgeting 31–4; DIY, repairs 35–7; money-saving tips 35–8; debt 33–4; maintenance 28–31; transport 72–4; travel 70–1

relationships: family and friends 7–13; marriage 1–3; romantic 14–16; stepfamilies 50–1

self-confidence, self-esteem 82–4

time-management 101–4